THE LOST RAILWAY LINES OF AYRSHIRE

Ayrshire Railway Walks

Alasdair Wham

A series of journeys along the many disused railway routes in Ayrshire. Lines that have closed and now pass, silent through countryside and town. These are journeys into the recent past with an eye on what remains today. Explore and discover the heritage that the railway era has left behind.

LOCAL HISTORY SERIES No 20

THE LOST RAILWAY LINES OF AYRSHIRE

Alasdair Wham

Dedicated to James Howie Wham M.M.

Illustrations by Kay Stevenson

ISBN 1 872350 27 5

Cover photographs
Memorial to Sister Laurienne,nr Commondyke
Inset: Remains of steam engine, Dunaskin
Photography by Alasdair Wham

Published & typeset by:
G.C. Book Publishers Ltd., North Main Street, Wigtown,
Scotland. DG8 9HL
Tel/fax 01988 40 2499
email: sales@gcbooks.demon.co.uk
web site: http://www.gcbooks.demon.co.uk

The Lost Railway Lines of Ayrshire

Introduction

Railway lines retain a fascination long after the last train has departed. Frequently overgrown, often neglected, a disused track offers glimpses into a way of life when roads were poor and railways were a vital lifeline. Like a narrow sliver of history a disused line can say a lot about those who built it and the communities it linked. If all that sounds too grand then exploring abandoned track beds is also a good way to get exercise and with less chance of getting lost than you have on a mountain top!

This is not a book about trains, their story is chronicled elsewhere. The journeys described are intended for the curious who maybe pass under an old railway bridge on their way to work and wonder why it was built or for the person who walks their dog along a crumbling railway embankment and wants to know something of the history of the abandoned line. Ayrshire provides many opportunities to satisfy their curiosity and to enjoy varied countryside and panoramic views.

The journeys through Ayrshire reveal a railways tradition which is a proud one, with its roots in the old waggonways, where horses dragged coal filled wagons. The county can even claim one of the earliest experiments with steam engines on the Duke of Portland's line between Troon and Kilmarnock. Nowadays Ayrshire can claim probably the oldest existing railway viaduct in the world, the recently restored Laigh Milton Viaduct. It also has the highest railway bridge in Britain, at one hundred and sixty-seven feet at Ballochmyle on the Kilmarnock to Dumfries line. This bridge also, for 51 years, held the world record for having the biggest stone arch at 181 feet! However Ayrshire's railways are not bound up in records but in the communities and the industries they served.

The railways have served Ayrshire for many generations, from carrying tourists to the seaside where steamers would take them for 'a trip doon the watter', to carting coal to iron furnaces. Not often glamorous but very vital. No famous or majestic engines breaking speed records, but steam, then diesel, engines often hauling lines of clanking coal wagons. By contrast the railway lines in Galloway often seem romanticised with images of the famous 'Paddies' speeding through the countryside.

The rail network in Ayrshire began with the opening of the Duke of Portland's Kilmarnock and Troon Railway in 1810. This should more accurately be known as a plateway for horse drawn wagons but which saw unsuccessful attempts by George Stephenson to introduce a steam engine, known as the Duke which proved too heavy for the rails. In 1831 the Ardrossan and Johnstone Railway, also using horse-drawn wagons, opened as far as Kilwinning but it was 1839 before the railway era really began in Ayrshire when the Glasgow, Paisley, Kilmarnock and Ayr Railway opened from Ayr to Irvine with a link from Dalry to Kilmarnock following in 1843.

By 1850 a line from Glasgow through Kilmarnock to Dumfries had been opened by the Glasgow, Dumfries and Carlisle Railway. with its opening, the GD&C railway was amalgamated with the GPK&A railway to form the Glasgow and South Western Railway, a company which dominated the railway routes of the county until the regrouping after the First World War which led to the London, Midland and Scottish Railway. Ayrshire was a railway battleground with fierce competition between the G&SW and its rival the Caledonian Railway who tried to break the G&SW monopoly of the coal trade in Ayrshire and gain access to the ports of Ayr, Troon and Ardrossan. Indeed, such was the rivalry that a line built at great expense, near Muirkirk, was never opened, and no train ever ran on it, because it would have allowed access to new markets to the other company.

A network of lines and branches grew throughout the county providing a lifeline for small and large communities, reaching east to Muirkirk in 1848, south to Girvan in 1860 and north to Largs in 1885. Many of the lines were linked to coal pits or iron furnaces. The railways carried coal to fuel both industry and home and generated a healthy export trade. New lines continued to be opened until the early years of this century. The last line to be opened, was the Maidens and Dunure Railway, in 1906, a bold but unsuccessful attempt to develop the tourist trade along the Carrick coast. The Golfers' Railway as it was known did however leave a fine legacy in the Turnberry Hotel. It was not long after the regrouping of the railways in 1923 that some lines were closed, a process which continued until the Beeching cuts in the 1960s.

In Ayrshire a major factor affecting the railways has been the transformation of the coal industry, with the end of deep coal mining in Ayrshire and its replacement by open cast operations. Small communities based on mining, like Glenbuck have literally disappeared along with a way of life often endured, rarely enjoyed, because of its unremitting harshness. With the demise of the coal industry and the effect of the Beeching cuts, the railway network has been savagely pruned. Cold economic reality has also doused many of the county's traditional industries, like iron and steel production and this also has had a knock-on effect on the railways. No longer do lines run east of Cumnock and many cross country routes such as the Kilmarnock to Dalry and Ayr to Cumnock have closed or been severely truncated.

The remnants of Ayrshire's railway today are based on commuter traffic but the carrying of coal is still important. The main line from Glasgow to Ayr, with its branch at Kilwinning to Ardrossan and Largs, is the busiest section carrying many passengers to the city and back and during the summer the tourist trade gives extra revenue to the line. South of Ayr the line continues via Girvan to Stranraer thus providing the only railway link to the Irish ferries since the closure of the 'Port Road'. Recently passenger traffic between Ayr and Kilmarnock has restarted using the cross-country route from Barassie to Kilmarnock and is being marketed as the 'Burns Line' an early sign that privatisation will bring new opportunities although only time will tell if privatisation will bring lasting benefits. Coal lines still exist with a branch from the Mauchline line at Annbank to the coal disposal point at Killoch and a branch from the Girvan line to an open cast mine near Dalmellington. The other surviving main route is from Glasgow via Kilmarnock to Dumfries and the south which is used mainly for freight but has seen stations at Auchinleck and New Cumnock reopen to encourage more passenger traffic.

The Ayrshire railway network is much changed but what remains is in reasonable health and may under privatisation even see a little growth with new links to open cast mining operations. It would appear that in Ayrshire railways and mines will always be linked.

The journeys in this book along the lost railway lines tell the story of why the lines were built and why they closed, but also show how important the railways were to the communities they served. It may also be the last opportunity to record the railway heritage left by the 'lost lines' before many of the railway sites become unrecognisable or simply fade away.

A word of caution, however, since the railways closed it is not always clear who owns the land. In many areas I suspect that British Rail and its successor Railtrack have sold the land to local landowners and farmers. I would advise you to seek the permission of the landowner where possible and to follow the Country Code. Please do not assume that because a walk is described in this book that anyone has given permission for you to follow in my footsteps.

It also important to keep off dangerous and disused structures, such as viaducts which have been closed to the public or to venture near old mine workings. Permission to walk these 'lost lines' will always depend on mutual trust and respect.

The walks vary in length and most can be shortened or completed in stages. It is advisable to have good walking boots and to be prepared for all weather. An ordnance survey map and a bus timetable are also handy. Take care on the lost routes and enjoy exploring Ayrshire's rich railway heritage.

Alasdair Wham,
Ayr,
February, 1997

Journey A

The Forgotten Line - The Golfers' Railway Today

A Trail of Caravans and Brambles

The view from the Doon Viaduct to the road bridge and the Auld Brig 'O Doon

The Golfers' Railway, today, is lying in a state of decay. Where once, there was a narrow ribbon of steel over eighteen miles in length connecting small villages along the Carrick coastline, now for long stretches there are only brambles choking the route of the abandoned Maidens and Dunure Light Railway. This small branch line left the main Girvan line at Alloway Junction and looped through the small villages of Dunure, Maidens and Turnberry before rejoining the main line near Girvan and was known as the 'Shore Road' to the railwaymen. The history of the railway, however, says much for the opportunism of the railway builders. It was built, not to exploït natural resources as so many of Ayrshire's lines were, but to develop a new market, that of the tourist. For that reason the Maidens and Dunure Light Railway was ahead of its time, a bold attempt to develop new business for the Glasgow and South Western Railway. Today something of the scenic attractions of the railway can still be glimpsed from walking the stretches of the disused trackbed, that are still recognisable.

Opened in May 1906 the Golfers' Railway, as it was better known, was used to attract business to the newly constructed Turnberry Hotel complete with its golf courses. Inevitably in Ayrshire, the Burns connection was used to sell the attractions of this remote line. The G&SW who built and initially ran the line, had ambitious plans to attract golfers from all over Britain to play over the seaside links and to enjoy the luxury of a top-class hotel complete with 'electric lights and modern sanitary fittings'. For many years the railway company ran special trains to encourage the use of the hotel. There was a regular sleeper service from Euston Station to Turnberry and each Saturday there were express services from Glasgow St Enoch for golfers. Turnberry Station was by far the grandest station on the line complete with glass canopy and covered walkway so that passengers could leave the train and reach the hotel without getting wet. The entrance to the hotel still faces inland towards the railway station although visitors today would be unaware of the connection.

A walk along the disused railway track, still possible in parts, shows the beauty of this part of Ayrshire with views west towards Arran and Kintyre, south to Ailsa Craig and Ireland beyond, and north towards Bute and Cowal. When combined with attractive seaside villages like Dunure and Maidens and attractive castles at Greenan, Dunure and Culzean some would argue that the line closed before it should have. They are wrong. The line never made a profit even before the age of the car. As early as 1930, only 25 years after the line opened and a few years after the regrouping of the railways which created the LMS, passenger services were withdrawn from the stretch between Ayr and Turnberry. Passengers going to Turnberry by rail had then to travel to Girvan. Even this arrangement lasted only until 1942 before the whole line was closed to passengers. Freight services still continued until 1955 when they ceased. From 1947, however, the line was reopened for passengers from Ayr as far as Butlins Holiday Camp at the Heads of Ayr. With the closure of this service in 1968 the track was lifted and all trains going south from Ayr had to travel via Maybole.

Usually when a line closes, the sections which pass through or near to towns are soon swallowed up and in the rural areas the lines can remain often untouched. With the M&D Railway, the opposite is true.

The best preserved part to walk today is near the beginning of the route where the M&D branched from the mainline near Alloway which in the last thirty years has seen extensive house building but surprisingly has left the route almost untouched. In the rural areas, however, many parts of the railway especially near stations have been developed into caravan parks as their new owners have taken advantage of the well drained sites and lines of caravans now extend along the trackbed where previously trains stood.

Our journey began near Alloway where travellers on the busy A77 bypass hardly notice the line of the old railway lost in trees, high on an embankment beside the road. Within half-a-mile the railway crosses the road into Alloway. Now only the abutments of the bridge remain but it is a convenient place to start the journey along the disused railway. The route passed through open fields when built but now Alloway has expanded hemming in the route from both sides. It passes under a recently widened road bridge at Doonholm Road and then a narrow cutting before reaching the first station.

Alloway Station was sited in a cutting next to Alloway Church and the ruined Auld Alloway Kirk. Recent housing developments at Robertson's Field to the north of the line have meant that an access road has been built across the line at the site of the station. A circular tunnel lined with a corrugated metal inlay, means that you can continue your journey without leaving the route. The station site is now unrecognisable from the pictures of the railway in its heyday. Nothing remains of the station with its island platform and signal box and the goods yard to the south of the station has been turned into the Tam O'Shanter Experience and the Burns National Heritage Park. Maybe this is Burns revenge for the railway by means of a tunnel, having passed underneath the graveyard at Auld Alloway Kirk where his father was buried and only a few hundred yards from his world famous cottage. The tunnel was originally square faced but the entrance has now been changed to match the recently built tunnel a few yards along the line. The tunnel leads to an elaborate Doon Viaduct over the River Doon. Complete with mock turrets, the bridge like the tunnel is still in good condition.

There are views of the road bridge and then further upstream the Auld Brig o' Doon where Tam O'Shanter's mare lost her tail fleeing from the witches in Burns' poem. This area is a major tourist attraction and one wonders how the railway obtained permission to build a station, tunnel and bridge at this point. The route then continues uninterrupted through a long deep cutting passing under a road bridge before emerging on an embankment with fields on one side with views to Newark Castle and the Carrick Hills and on the other side modern housing pressing against the route until the site of the road bridge at the A719, now infilled, where the A719 crossed the railway. Situated here were Greenan Castle sidings with two small sidings which appeared to have been only used to collect the early potatoes from nearby farms. Beside the track at this point was claimed to be the tallest telephone pole in Scotland, needed to carry the wires over the road at the bridge! Greenan Castle, which the sidings are named after, is perched precariously on a cliff top by the sea about a mile away.

It is pleasing to note that work is being done to restore the drainage on this stretch and allow walkers to enjoy a quiet pathway away from the busyness of the roads. This is the easiest part of the line to walk and South Ayrshire Council and their predecessors are to be commended on the work they have done to preserve the route and to provide a footpath for local residents.

On the other side of the A719 the trackbed is marshy and the drainage ruined by the infilling of the bridge. From here it is only half-a-mile to the site of a missing bridge and the security fence at Butlin's Wonderwest Holiday Camp. The walker is forced to retrace his steps to the A719 and to pass the camp and pick-up the line beyond the Heads of Ayr Farm Park. Within the holiday camp, however, was the site of the Heads of Ayr Station which was the last station to close on the line with 'special trains' depositing the holidaymakers during the summer season. The station consisted of a long platform with a small white concrete building. Campers went from here by covered walkway to the camp itself. Like many other station sites on this railway, it has now been landscaped into a caravan park. A mile further on at the Heads of Ayr Caravan Park was another station of the same name. Of this second Heads of Ayr Station, nestling in the lee of the Heads of Ayr, only part of the platform remains lost among the caravans.

My favourite section of the railway route to walk is beyond the Heads of Ayr Caravan Park where the trackbed is carried high on an embankment across the fields, before it winds passed Bracken Bay and on towards Dunure. Pause just before you reach a deep cutting hewn out of the hillside and look back over Bracken Bay and the cliffs of the Heads of Ayr towards the town of Ayr. The view is spectacular stretching in all directions from the mountains of Arran to the hills above Ardrossan and many hills inland. However from here until Dunure much of the line has been lost, re-ploughed into the fields.

The site of Dunure Station with its island platform, which was accessed from the road bridge at the end of the platform, remains increasingly overgrown and used as a dump for garden refuse. Dunure Station was at the top of a steep hill where Station Road crosses the old railway by a bridge. The station is about half-a mile from the harbour. Like many stations built before the age of the car, passengers were made to walk to catch their train. Beyond the station there is a rubbish filled cutting difficult to walk along but eventually the route crosses Dunduff Burn by a girder bridge. The railway passed behind the village of Dunure high above Dunure Castle providing many fine views before entering a deep cutting before it crossed the road again. The drainage in this cutting has broken down making it very difficult to walk. A pleasant stretch then rewards the walker as the line passes through fields before reaching the next obstacle, the missing Croy Viaduct.

Trains on the Maidens and Dunure Light Railway to give it its full title were restricted to 25mph. This speed restriction saved on construction costs. Despite this, two substantial viaducts were built over the Croy and Rancleugh Glens. The optical illusion of the electric brae at Croy also applied to the trains which could climb away from the Croy Viaduct with seemingly little effort. Pass the electric brae and keep to the road as the route stops abruptly at the site of the former viaduct which is next to a deep glen. The route can be regained by following the road to Croy Shore. At the first caravan park down this road is the site of Knoweside Station which was to the west of the road.

Beyond Knoweside Station there is another stretch of fairly easy walking leading to the Rancleugh Viaduct which reached a height of 125 feet. Its pillars which once supported a metal girder structure are all that remain, an object of curiosity to travellers on the nearby road. Balchriston Halt on the far side of Rancleugh Viaduct was near a cottage. Traces of a platform still remain. Serving a sparse population, these stops hardly saw any passengers and were of more use to farmers loading produce.

After the halt there is a long cutting leading to the second and final tunnel on the route. From here the route can be followed through woods which lead to the grounds of Culzean Castle run by the National Trust for Scotland. Culzean Castle was never open to the public when the trains ran through its grounds. A small station nestling among the trees served the Marquis of Ailsa whose support was essential for the building of the railway. The station which was officially called Glenside but better known to locals as the Marquis's Station is now landscaped into the Culzean Caravan and Camping site. The platform remains, on which a piper sometimes plays, although one suspects that the piper is used more as a tourist bait rather than to lament the passing of the railway. Culzean Castle and Country Park with it's eighteenth century castle and grounds, a major tourist attraction, contains the next part of the line. Close by the entrance to the Country Park and starting near the picnic site at Kennelmount, a stretch of the disused track has been turned into a path for walkers. Again the views are compelling, over the castle grounds towards Ailsa Craig and across the firth to Arran and Kintyre. It is not difficult to see why Culzean Castle is such a big tourist attraction. Unfortunately it is too late to benefit the railway.

Leaving the Castle grounds, a very overgrown stretch makes the journey towards the next station at Maidens difficult. Maidens Station is sited about half-a-mile from the village where the railway crossed over the A719. Steep steps still lead up from the road to the site of the station but like many on this line it is now a caravan park with no trace of the station remaining. The station was a modest affair consisting of a wooden building with two overhanging canopies.

In just over a mile you reach the woods that lead to Turnberry Hotel and the site of the station of the same name. On the way, the site of the old wartime airfield is clearly seen beside the lighthouse overlooking the famous Turnberry golf course scene of many a classic golfing encounter. A detour to reach the site of the station is necessary because of the dense undergrowth. The hotel has long outgrown the railway and a search is required to find the concrete edge of the station platform which is embedded in the ground - unnoticed since the age of car and helicopter arrived at Turnberry! However, one part of the station does remain in use - in 1957 the former platform roof was sold to Dumbarton FC, where it was erected at what is known as the Overwood Drive end. At least the Ayr United fans should feel at home when they visit Dumbarton's ground.

Ailsa Craig is even more visible as the track turns south. Hills mask the route from the busy A77 although the sound of the traffic is never totally lost. The sight of the final station on the line is reached and the former goods yard at Dipple is occupied by a caravan site! Beyond here the going gets tough. A deep cutting infilled with rubbish blocks the way and another detour is necessary. The nearby A77 provides the only way forward. Near Chapeldonan the route can be picked up again and as the route winds finally towards Girvan it passes a recently built industrial estate. It is the first sign of industry spotted on the route and of course didn't exist when the railway was open. Lack of industry was yet another reason why the line was never financially viable. It takes a lot of early potatoes to make a line profitable.

Just before Girvan, the M&D R joined the main line again and so ended a little used branch line, now assigned a footnote in the history of railways in Scotland. Nature is reclaiming what was a bold attempt to develop business in this area. Only two small sections have been preserved and for that South Ayrshire Council and the National Trust for Scotland are to be commended. Other than these sections most of the old route is sadly disappearing fast, choked by brambles. The Golfers' Railway, however, did leave a fine legacy of championship golf courses but few golfers today will appreciate the debt that they owe to the now departed railway.

The former railway embankment near the Heads of Ayr

Main features:

A1 **Alloway Junction**: 349 188 The signal box has been removed. Housing encroaches onto the site. A few hundred yards from this point, on the far side of the A77 there used to be a short branch to the Glengall Siding (353 184) at Ailsa Hospital.

A2 **Alloway Station:** 334 181 The Burns connection is the attraction which makes this area a must on the tourist trail with the Burns National Heritage Park beside the former station site.

A3 **Greenan Castle Sidongs**: 314 183 Located next to the infilled road bridge.

A4 **Heads of Ayr Station:** 285 180 The original station of this name not the one in the nearby holiday camp. A fine stretch of embankment, carried the railway west from here. (Heads of Ayr Station in Butlin's Holiday Camp: 302 183)

A5 **Dunure Station:** 263 167 The island platform can still be recognised.

A6 **Croy Viaduct:** 252 130 Dismantled and hard to reach, itcrossed a deep gully - be careful! A detour is necessary. Knoweside Station was just west of the viaduct: 254 127

A7 **Rancleugh Viaduct**: 254 114 The piers remain impressive. To the west of the site was Balchriston Halt.

A8 **Glenside Station:** 242 098 Now part of a caravan site situated near the entrance to Culzean Castle and Country Park.

A9 **Maidens Station:** 222 079 Situated near the abutments of a rail bridge over the A719.

A10 **Turnberry Station**: 206 057 The front of the hotel faced the railway: the rear of the hotel faces the sea.

A11 **Dipple Goods Station**: 204 023 Another caravan site

A12 **Junction**: 196 993 From the nearby road the junction with the Maybole to Girvan line can still be seen.

Journey B

The Doon Valley Railway

Looking north towards Dunaskin

Don't get too excited but there still is a railway that runs through the Doon Valley. Admittedly it is only a mineral line and it ends at an opencast coalfield but for most of its journey it follows the old railway route to Dalmellington. There are even plans to use part of the line from Minnivey, near Dalmellington to Dunaskin where the old iron works of the Dalmellington Iron Company (DICo) have been opened as an industrial museum. The Scottish Industrial Railway Centre operated by the Ayrshire Railway Preservation Group hope to run steam trains from Minnivey near Dalmelligton where they have their centre, to Dunaskin where a heritage centre has been opened. At Dunaskin a new station has been built and at Minnivey developments including a new platform have also been completed. Passengers could be carried along the valley for the first time since 1964 when the passenger services to Dalmellington were finally withdrawn,

The history of the railways in this valley began with a grand scheme to build a railway to Galloway, but when this was abandoned the discovery of ironstone and coal deposits led to the development of a railway network.

The Glasgow and Belfast Union Railway intended to build a branch from Belmont then a farm outside Ayr, now a heavily built up area, to Smithston Farm a distance of eight miles. From here the Ayrshire and Galloway Railway wanted to build a line to Dalmellington and then through the hilly region south of Dalmellington to Galloway. While the Doon Valley caused few problems to railway engineers, the hilly region south of the Doon Valley was too big a barrier and plans had to be modified. The railway never got south of Dalmellington.

However, the Act of Parliament which gave the go-ahead to build a railway between Smithston Farm and Dalmellington along with the plans for a connecting railway to Ayr gave the Houldsworth family, who already owned iron furnaces in Lanarkshire, the green light to develop iron works at Dunaskin, three miles north of Dalmellington. In a few short years the valley was transformed with the construction of coal mines and ironstone pits with a rail network linking the pits to the iron works. By 1848 the Dalmellington Iron Company (DICo) was in production. There was, however, one major problem - the railway to Ayr had not been completed. All the materials needed to construct the iron works and the limestone which had to be brought in for the smelting had to be delivered by road. The pig iron had to be carried away in a similar fashion. To the Houldsworth family it was a recipe for frustration and financial loss. Even plans to build a railway to link the iron furnaces to coal mines further south at Sillyhole, near Dalmellington were delayed by the A&G Railway who were short of funds and even shorter of courage to develop their project. It took until the 7th November 1848 for the section between Drumgrange Just north of Dunaskin and Sillyhole to be completed with the section near Sillyhole, which was marshy, proving difficult.

If the A&G Railway's plans had not progressed sufficiently then the G&B Union Railway's progress was worse. It had not started. It took the involvement of a third railway, the Glasgow and South Western, to make headway. A new Act of Parliament led to the demise of the A&G and the beginning of the Ayr and Dalmellington Railway run by the G&SW. Building started in 1854 with the A&D linking with the G&SW line at what is now Falkland Junction in Ayr and stretching over 13 miles south to Dalmellington. The line opened on 15th May 1856 and by the 7th August in the same year a passenger service had begun.

The railway from Ayr also carried the line to Maybole. The A&D left what became the mainline to Girvan via Maybole at Dalrymple Junction which was near Pleasantfield Farm and headed south east crossing the sixteen arch Burnton Viaduct (Dalrymple Viaduct) built of stone from quarries at Dunaskin. Near the viaduct a branch line to Coylton left at Potterston Junction named after a nearby farm. It was a mineral line allowing the DICo to take coal from their pits near Coylton to their furnaces, a distance of over five and a half miles. The A&D line continued towards Hollybush where there was a station. A mile beyond Hollybush Station the railway reached Holehouse Junction by means of a high embankment bisecting the fields. At Holehouse Junction there was a branch line to Belston Junction connecting there to the Ayr and Cumnock Line. At Holehouse Junction there was also an exchange platform for passengers. The line continued south passing through Patna where there was another station and then reached the iron furnaces at Dunaskin where Waterside Station was located. Dunaskin was the name by which the Post Office called the area after a nearby farm but to confuse matters the railway called the area Waterside after another nearby farm. From here the railway reached Dalmellington and the final station. To steam trains the route was a steep climb from Ayr.

Today the Coylton and Holehouse Branches have been closed. The line south of Waterside was closed in 1964 but a line runs to Minnivey to collect coal from the opencast workings. It is this part which the Ayrshire Railway Preservation Group intend to use for their steam excursions. To the walker of old lines there are three main parts to explore - the Coylton Line, the Holehouse Branch (described in journey C) and the section between Waterside and Dalmellington. In addition traces of many older lines around Dunaskin still exist connecting closed pits to the main railway line through the valley.

The Coylton Line - the Nanny Line

The line to Coylton was opened in the mid-1860s and was used to supply coal from pits in the Sundrum Estate near Coylton, to the furnaces at Dunaskin. The junction still can be seen today leaving the main line a few hundred yards south of Burnton Viaduct. Originally there was a signal box to control the rail traffic at Potterson Junction. At the beginning of the Coylton Line, the disused track is wide enough to suggest sidings but it soon narrows as it enters the first cutting. The track while overgrown is in surprisingly good shape. A missing bridge which allowed the farmer to move between his fields is no obstacle and the route of the former railway is easily followed for the first section until the road to the farm is reached. Beyond the farm track it disappears for a short time but can be found again where there used to be a siding at Purclewan with a water tank situated east of the minor road linking the B742 to the A713 close to the old corn mill of the same name. The line can be traced back into the woods to the west of the road and then can be followed east towards the A713 where the road crosses a bridge over the line. The railway then headed to the south of Martnaham Loch where there was a level crossing at the junction of two minor roads, a water tank and sidings to a local sawmill. The route then took the railway south of Raithhill Farm and under the Ayr to Cumnock road to the pits. The line was used to supply coal until the mines closed. It must have been expensive to maintain and herein lies a puzzle. At its eastern extremity the railway lay very close to the Ayr and Cumnock Line which was opened just after this railway was built. The builders of the line must have known that the other line was going to open. Why didn't they wait? A short spur would have connected the pits to the A&C line and then via Belston Junction and Holehouse Junction the coal could have been taken to Dunaskin. The coal would, however, have been taken for a longer distance on G&SW lines. Did this make the building of the spur line unattractive? The G&SW knew how to charge for carriage. They were not cheap.

Locally the line was known as the 'Nanny Line', Nanny being the nickname of one of the first drivers on the line, whose real name was Thomas Rutherford and his engine became known as the 'Coylton Nanny'. The line was closed by 1935.

Waterside to Dalmellington

The Dunaskin Heritage Centre is well worth a visit. The industrial past of this valley is still etched in bricks and stones built into the side of the hill. The two tall chimneys, at 143 feet and 160 feet high, effortlessly dominate the surroundings. Mighty stone buildings used at various times to make iron or latterly bricks are the more impressive when you realise that most of materials were dragged here over pot-holed tracks. Pause at the bridge which crosses the railway line and leads to the heritage centre. Looking north, Waterside Station can be seen. The platform and signal box have gone but the distinctive spiral staircase at the rear of the building leading to the upper storey remains. To the west the remains of the slag heap reduced in size during the seventies, when it was used for bottoming roads still leaves an ugly scar - a blot on the landscape. To the east is the site of the blast furnaces built against a massive retaining wall which has survived although the furnaces have long gone. This arrangement allowed for the raw materials to be tipped in from the top. Limestone, iron ore (latterly imported from Spain) and uniquely coal were mixed. Coal could be used instead of coke, an advantage because the local blackband ironstone was rich in carbon. In operation the furnaces must have lit up the valley and the roar of the furnaces must have been heard for miles around. I imagine the smells also carried for miles! By 1921 iron production had ceased and by 1931 the Dalmellington Iron Company had been taken over by Bairds and a new company Bairds and Dalmellington created which further developed the Dalmellington coalfield.

The railway trail within the centre leads past the engine sheds to the newly built brick platform and waiting room. The steam train journey will take you two miles along the mineral line to Minnivey from here when opened. The journey along the old line to Dalmellington is a mile longer and the disused track can be accessed most easily from behind a bus shelter on the A713 opposite the Waterside Day Care Centre and a row of former miners' cottages. Evidence of railway sidings dominates the start of the walk with several concrete sleepers still in situ. The disused track is separated from the mineral line by a fence before the mineral line veers away south-east. Bridge number 26, with pillars constructed of bricks is soon reached. The bridge carries an access road to a nearby farm. The walking is pleasant with no obstacles as the track gradually pulls away from the road. Looking back towards the heritage centre the tall chimneys still dominate the scene along with the slag heap. The River Doon can be seen twisting its way along the valley. An image of a man with a glass bottomed box searching for pearls at this part which I had seen on an old cine film came back to mind. I can't imagine that he had much success as the river must have been very polluted.

Another road bridge to a farm crossed the line before a deep cutting. On the west side of the valley there were several farms. On the east side the present day operations of the coal industry were evident. A large opencast coalfield was clawing at the hillside, large dumper trucks working even on a Saturday. Another missing bridge and we reached the opencast coalfield. An infilled cutting over which a tarmac road had been built led directly to the coalfield. Once passed the new road, the cutting returned with views ahead to Dalmellington which expanded as the former railway started over marshland on an embankment. The hills looked formidable to the south. No wonder that the railway stopped in this valley. To the east was Minnivey, the centre of the Scottish Industrial Railway Centre and beyond that on a newly levelled field a tractor was at work reclaiming the land and covering the scar of the opencast working. The scene was almost changing as we watched the opencast coalfield making its planned progression north up the valley. Rarely can geography be so dynamic.

Between the disused railway route and the road there was a small loch created by flooded mine workings. This was the area of the Sillyhole mines closed by the late 1860s due to flooding. All around this area there had been coal mining. Across the railway line there had been at this point an aerial rope-way carrying coal from the Bogton mine on the west of the A713 to the coal washing plant at Burnton next to Minnivey which operated between 1930 and 1950. Also, on the far side of the road was Bogton Loch, part of a protected wetlands area where winter wildfowl breed. This was the scene of a wartime folly. An airfield was planned for a school of aerial gunnery which was going to use nearby Loch Doon as a target area where it was hoped to build a monorail system to carry targets for the planes to aim at. The monorail was never finished, the peat bogs preventing completion. If they had listened to the experiences of the railway builders near Sillyhole, they would have known of the problems. This part of the railway had been difficult to build, as the materials kept disappearing into the local bogs.

The site of Sillyhole signal box was then approached, requiring a short detour to a road bridge to cross a burn feeding into the River Doon. The low abutments of the rail bridge could still be seen set in the banks of the burn and beyond the burn the signalman's house now much extended is easily identified. The railway route now became a track used by townsfolk, skirting the back of a council estate until it reached the Doon Academy school grounds. Beyond the school grounds were some industrial units which cover the site of the former station which consisted of a single platform and simple stone buildings. This was the journey's end.

Dalmellington's main claim to fame lies in its coal mining past but it was also the birthplace of D. L. Smith, a most remarkable man, whose knowledge of the railways and industry of this valley and of the railways of south-west Scotland were so vividly captured in his writings. He told the story of 'The Dalmellington Iron Company' and of 'The Little Railways of South-West Scotland' with a rare insight into the lives of the people he worked with. Now sadly out of print, his books, if you can find a copy in a library or a second-hand bookshop are worth reading. All who attempt to chronicle the railways and the history of the people in this area owe him a debt.

The journey between the heritage centre and Dalmellington is certainly not demanding and the route has not been destroyed by re-developments until the last few hundred yards. The walk neatly links the industrial past of this valley, which the trains helped to serve. Clever planning will allow you to take the steam train back to Dunaskin when the line opens.

Waterside Station

Main features: .

B1 **Potterson Branch**: 377 152 The branch to Coylton left the main line here.
Fine views to the Burnton or Dalrymple Viaduct.

B2 Site where the railway crossed the minor road next to Purclewan Mill: 382 158

B3 Site where the railway crossed the minor road at the east end of Martnaham Loch: 405 177

B4 **Hollybush Station**: 392 149 Closed. The station building remains

B5 **Holehouse Junction:** 407 136 Start of the Rankinston Line See Journey C

B6 **Patna Station site:** 417 108 Don't bother looking

B7 **Waterside Station:** 437 086 Platform and buildings have gone, building remains

B8 **Dunaskin Heritage Centre:** 440 084 Industrial Museum open most of the year. Well worth a visit with interesting walks around the site and a countryside trail. Old railways abound.

B9 **Start of the walk to Dalmellington:** 443 083 The walk starts behind the bus shelter .

B10 **Loch Doon Aerial Gunnery School Light Railway:** 474 059 A light railway was built to connect Dalmellington to the project and it can still be traced. The railway ran through the Graigengillan Estate and stopped at Dalfarson a mile from the loch because to go further would have required a long tunnel.

B10 **Dalmellington Station**: 478 059 Site now occupied by light industrial units.

B12 **Minnivey:** 475 073 Site of the Scottish Industrial Railway Centre. Clearly signposted from the main road. Holds open days during the summer. Well worth a visit particularly when the steam train rides to Dunaskin get underway.

Journey C

Coal Lines

The Ayr and Cumnock and Rankinston Branches

Viaduct at Rankinston

The next two abandoned lines take us further east towards Cumnock in our journeys. The Rankinston and the Ayr and Cumnock lines opened about the same time towards the end of 1872 and both existed to serve the coal mines although passenger traffic and freight from other areas could be routed along them. The Ayr and Cumnock line left the Ayr to Mauchline Line at Annbank and cut across country passing through Cumnock and reaching Cronberry where it joined with the Auchinleck to Muirkirk line. The Rankinston Branch linked the Dalmellington line to the Ayr and Cumnock.

The A&C line snaked south-east until it joined with the Rankinston line at Belston Junction from where it headed east towards Cumnock. In Cumnock it passed under the Kilmarnock to Dumfries line at right angles and then headed north-east towards Cronberry Junction which was situated in the bleak moorland of Airds Moss. The total distance was over fifteen miles. It was a coal line with little passenger traffic most of which was shuttling miners to different mines along the route.

Today the A&C line exists as far as Drongan from where a new line has been built to carry coal traffic from the Killoch Disposal Point to the east of Drongan. Annbank Station at Annbank Junction has been closed with no sign of its wooden station building on the Ayr and Cumnock Branch or the wedge shaped platforms at the junction of the A&C and the Ayr and Mauchline Line, a cross-country route which is still open. The railway crosses the river Ayr over the Enterkine Viaduct as it heads south-east towards Drongan. There are no remains of Trabboch Station, opened in July 1896, which served the miners of Drumdow Colliery and Trabboch Colliery and which was located between the viaduct and Drongan Station.

Drongan Station with its passing loop was known as the Crewe of the North - an exaggeration but one which underlined the importance of this Ayrshire rail network founded on coal. Opened in 1876 the station played a vital role in the life of the village before the advent of a bus service. For local farmers it was a means of getting milk to creameries in Glasgow and to the people of Drongan it was how newspapers, mail and goods were delivered. The station closed partly due to problems with subsidence from a nearby mine which meant a speed restriction at the station of 5mph. The station buildings remain and are now an attractive private residence. The goods yard further to the south of the station is now used by a builder's merchant. Between Drongan and Belston Junction the line has largely disappeared, reclaimed by local farms.

The Rankinston Branch was about six miles in length and along its length there were several mines. Again there was little passenger traffic and with the closing of the mines its fate was sealed.

I found it easier to walk the Rankinston Branch from Holehouse Junction to Belston Junction and then head towards Drongan to catch a bus, and following the A&C line until it disappeared. The next walk I began at Belston Junction and walked to Cumnock leaving the stretch to Cronberry Junction to another day. It is up to the walker to decide how to plan the journeys.

There appears to be confusion over what the initials A&C represent. While on the maps it is referred to as the Ayr and Cumnock Line, some people refer to it as the Ayr and Cronberry Line, others the Annbank and Cumnock Line. There is logic in all these choices, maybe that is why many refer to it simply as the A&C.

The Rankinston Branch
From Holehouse Junction to Belston Junction.

The Rankinston Branch linked the Ayr to Dalmellington Line to the Ayr and Cumnock Line. While some of the countryside is scarred with coal bings the views to the north and west are panoramic. On a clear day some of the Perthshire hills are visible and the peaks of Arran to the west are always spectacular. The line joined with the Dalmellington Branch at Holehouse Junction and with the A&C line at Belston Junction. While hardly names which fire the imagination of railway enthusiasts, Holehouse Junction and Belston Junction are filled with memories for those who worked the line shuttling coal or carrying the occasional passenger.

Holehouse Junction found on the opposite side of the track from the A713 just north of Waterside, was an exchange platform complete with signal box. Passengers couldn't buy tickets but could be dropped off to wait for a connecting train. The site was reached by walking under the rail bridge and could be traced until near where it merged with the present line. The wedge shaped platform has been removed along with the signal box.

The first part of the abandoned route took us on an embankment passed Holehouse Farm. The bridges had been removed making progress slow and gorse grew thick on the line. However once passed the farm, the trackbed was clear and made for pleasant walking. The outline of where the sleepers had been was still noticeable in places. A bank of yellow primroses adding a splash of colour near one of the red sandstone abutments and the overall impression was one of tranquillity.

Beyond the Craigs of Kyle and a disused quarry on the other side of the valley in which we now found ourselves, the jagged Arran peaks rose with Browncarrick and Mochrum Hill further to the west. Just as we clocked up our first mile we entered a deep cutting. Sheep gathered as interested spectators looking down from the top of the bank. There were the remains of a railway hut halfway along the otherwise deserted cutting.

We emerged from the cutting into the idyllic setting of Kerse Loch. Three men were sitting in a boat fishing alone with their lines and their thoughts. There was a new fishing club hut to the west of the loch linked to the road by a narrow track. Ahead lay the abutment of a bridge and beyond the first glimpse of the coal bing near Rankinston. Between the cutting and the abutment the embankment had been removed, creating for the first time on this walk, boggy conditions underfoot. The abutment marked the beginning of the disused line as a track used by walkers. The line then curved to the right with ever increasing views to the east.

Once through an elaborate overbridge Knockshinnoch Farm lay to the left. Here there was a remarkable change in the layout. Once the railway had approached the B730 high on an embankment and crossed the road near a row of miners' cottages. Next to the bridge had been Cairntable Halt with its wooden platform. Now the landscape had been radically altered making it hard to imagine what it once looked like. The embankment and bridge had gone along with the miners' cottages. At the site of the bridge a farm gate now led into a field with cattle grazing contentedly. Only the ever dominant and obvious bing at Rankinston reminds you of this area's true heritage. Crossing the road, the trackbed is soon rejoined as it nears a road bridge over it. Here earth and sand has been pushed onto the line narrowing it. Passing through a fence built across the line a beautiful sandstone bridge crosses the Bow Burn. To the south near the summit of Bow Hill were Bowhill Ironstone Pits, Numbers 1 and 2, closed in 1913, which were connected by a mineral line to the Dalmellington Branch.

The approach to Rankinston was bleak. The ground carried the scars of the closed Littlemill Mine. A bridge carrying a railway over the trackbed we were walking on towards the site of former brickworks hinted at the industrial activity that there was once in this area. A branch railway on a steep incline which had originally led to ironstone pits was also located here. In front of us was Rankinston consisting of several rows of council houses at right angles to the former railway track. There were the remains of several tracks at this point with the line we were following having been landscaped into playing fields. Over on the other side of the road through Rankinston was the site of the station of which no trace remained. Rankinston Station had opened to passengers on New Year's Day 1884.

The line now passed over two substantial viaducts before reaching another cutting. The first viaduct reaching to 150 feet was the scene of a bizarre incident in the summer of 1996 when a dog jumped the wall not realising that there was a seventy foot drop at that point. The dog who should be called 'Lucky' only injured a leg. Be careful as you would not likely be as fortunate.

Cutting followed by embankment, all well-preserved, with the occasional missing bridge, formed the pattern until we reached Sinclairston. The views to the north were panoramic and along with the distant Perthshire Hills, could be seen the Ailsa shipyard at Troon, Prestwick Airport and Coylton. We were ever conscious of the planes circling to land at Prestwick some of which seemed to use Rankinston main street to navigate by. Near Sinclairston we discovered some of the groundframe for Polquhairn Pit and to the south more coal bings. Sinclairston itself was a pretty village with the school found right beside the trackbed.

Drumsmodden Farm lay ahead and beyond that the site of Belston Junction. Here the Rankinston joined the Ayr and Cumnock Line (A&C). Along this stretch 'the twins' as the double-engined Littlemill Colliery train was known, would arrive with its load of coal trucks to be shunted to Falkland Junction in Ayr.

At the junction, once very busy, we found no sign of the signalbox or the watercolumn. The watercolumn had been very important not just for the trains but also for the people of Drumsmudden (Drumsmodden is the modern spelling) whose water supply often ran dry. The water supply for Belston came from Rankinston and it was possible for a man at Sinclairston to open a valve to let water run down to a burn near Drumsmudden where it could be collected.

Here we turned back towards Drongan along the A&C line. At regular positions beside the track, there were inspection holes in the ground with the covers removed, which exposed an underground pipe which could have carried an additional water supply to the junction. After a missing bridge the track continued until we reached a section which had been used as a dumping ground for broken concrete. To the south, here had been Drumsmudden Colliery which was closed by 1904. No sign of the colliery or the nearby miners' row remained. Just beyond here the trackbed stopped suddenly at a sandstone abutment. On the other side of the road, a minor road which linked the B7046 to the A70, the embankment had been removed along with all traces of the line. In the distance the railway to Killoch Colliery could be spotted but our track had disappeared. We continued to walk on passing by Whitehill farm without seeing any further signs of the former railway until we reached Drongan.

Belston Junction to Cumnock

A full car park beside Belston Loch suggested a fishing competition in progress. Certainly everyone was too busy fishing to pay any attention to the two walkers dropped by car and quickly crossing the fields away from the loch. The disused Ayr to Cumnock railway just beside Belston Loch and the site of Belston Junction was soon reached.

At Belston Junction there was a marked contrast to the scene at the nearby loch and what the junction must have been like when the line was operational. Now at the junction all was silence. A few trees had sprouted from the embankment and beneath them sat an old bath, a watering tank for a herd of cattle. It was difficult to believe that this rail junction buried deep in the Ayrshire countryside had once been a busy and important junction for the surrounding rail system. Trains, mainly coal trains, approached from the Rankinston Line and from the Drongan direction passing at this junction. From the other direction, Cumnock and our destination today, coal trains also approached Belston Junction. The junction must have been alive to the sound of straining steam engines and clanking coal wagons with the water tank, mounted on a frame much in use to replenish thirsty tanks.

The trackbed was clearly defined and even the drainage remained good, ensuring firm ground, as we started towards Cumnock, several stations away along the Ayr to Cumnock Line. Our first stopping place we had planned at the site of Ochiltree Station about two miles away. Only cattle were curious as to what we were doing as we strode along. We found it difficult to pass under the minor road bridge because of the muddy conditions at High Plyde where the drainage had failed and took the easy way out climbing up to the road crossing it and carefully working our way down the steep slope of the cutting on the other side. The cutting soon became an embankment before we reached the site of a missing rail bridge beside a road junction. Another scramble and we were across. Before entering the next cutting we noticed another disused track approaching from the south on a low embankment. This was from a local mine now closed. The cutting became wider where the lines joined. The line was then crossed by another bridge before we reached the first major engineering works in this section, the eleven arched sandstone viaduct over the Burnock Water. The structure looked very sound its grandeur masked by trees growing around it, making it difficult to get a good view of the complete structure. The viaduct must have been over a hundred feet high where it crossed the narrow stream.

We had still not reached Ochiltree Station but we could see the village lying to the north over a mile away. At the next farm we passed under another sandstone bridge and in the distance beside the next road bridge we saw Ochiltree Station. The buildings to the left of the track had been extended but the original buildings remained. Given the distance from the village and the lack of passenger trains it could hardly have been overused. Prior to the First World War, the Caledonian Railway ran Edinburgh to Ayr passenger trains through here twice a day. Maybe it was a ploy by the G&SW to reduce profitability for their bitter rivals!

Another cutting opened, quickly becoming an embankment, again affording expansive views to the north. The television transmitter at Darvel was prominent and closer to us the pithead at the Barony Colliery one of the last deep mines to close in Ayrshire. Auchinleck, its secondary school exposed on the top of a hill was also before us. To the west, towards the coast could be seen Killoch Colliery and Ochiltree. The peaks of Arran usually visible were today shrouded in clouds.

There was a further road bridge and then a section where a woodland had seeded itself over the line with the usual effects - trees growing tall and spindly competing for the light. As we left the shelter of the trees the first of several heavy showers reached us. Hurrying on, we sought the shelter of the next wood which lay just ahead. Here we encountered difficult conditions underfoot before emerging at the site of Skares Station next to a road bridge. Any sign of the station, opened in July 1901, with its sidings had gone, with a few half-completed brick houses now occupying the site. The village of Skares, a mining village lay over a mile to the south with the remains of the Whitehill Colliery between the station and the village. Beyond the station there were more problems to overcome as the line had been used as a dump.

Shortly after Skares Station there was a large seven arch sandstone viaduct. The first arch crossed a minor road the others once led the railway over Ward Burn. This section was known as Dykes Junction. Here the Dykes and Hindsward Railway, approached from the south, feeding coal wagons onto the line from local pits in the early part of the century before these mines closed around 1925. The largest pit and the last to close in the area was the Whitehill Colliery, which was still in operation until 1966. As we neared Dumfries House Station there was evidence of more branches merging with the A&C line and of more sidings.

Dumfries House Station and railway cottages were situated to the west of a road bridge and to the north of the line and served the large house of the same name about a mile to the north and on the other side of the busy A70 Cumnock to Ayr road. A long straight tree lined road known as Station Avenue had connected the station to the house. It was not surprising to discover that the owner of the house was no more successful in getting the railway to pass his doorstep than the inhabitants of Ochiltree and Skares. Given the lack of population in the surrounding area, I was intrigued to discover that in 1889 offers were invited for a five or seven year lease to run a bookstall at the station. One wonders if anyone tendered for it!

The importance of coal to this line was very evident, when a third of a mile beyond Dumfries House Station there were further signs of mineral lines feeding into the line, this time from Knockterra Coal Pit, which closed in 1914. Beyond Rose Burn, however, there was no sign of the miners' row at Garrallan which had once been beside the line. As we approached Cumnock the line of route of the railway became increasingly indistinct, more overgrown, and eventually swallowed up by the B7046 which had shadowed the railway line albeit sometimes from a distance since the start of our journey. However, the line quickly re-emerged on a high embankment just beyond Changue Farm, separating again from the road. Bravely we walked the overgrown route only to be stopped by a missing bridge. It was very difficult to climb down and then mount the other side and hardly worth the effort for the few yards which existed beyond it. Strictly for the enthusiasts! The Glengyron miners' row which was situated to the south of the embankment had been demolished and had become an overgrown wilderness. From there we kept to a field as we skirted another farm with the ominous sign painted on one wall of the farmhouse claiming 'white power'. At this point the railway had passed by Glengyron Mine with several sidings. Again, there was nothing left to indicate anything of the railway or mine. Suddenly we emerged above the Cumnock bypass. The bypass has been cut deeply through the very high embankment of the former railway as it entered the town. A steep climb on the other side of the bypass led to a few hundred yards of very exposed embankment on what had become a walkway for nearby residents. To the north of the former line and immediately below the embankment lay a housing estate. To the south was an industrial estate specialising in clothes - Falmer's jeans and the Sweater Shop. The route descended to road level and was immediately lost to housing developments. Studying the map suggested that the line had continued to the north of the cemetery towards a viaduct. Right enough through blocks of flats we spotted an impressive viaduct and crossing the main road we reached a path which ascended quickly to the height of the viaduct. The embankment leading up to the viaduct had been removed with blocks of flats following the former route of the railway. The impression created was of the viaduct stopping dramatically at the level of the top of the flats.

To the north of the cemetery on the approach to the viaduct, high on the now removed embankment was the site of the single platformed Cumnock (A&C) Station sometimes known just as Cumnock Station. With the building of flats and landscaping it was difficult to visualise the scene as it must have been in the heyday of the railway.

The viaduct another impressive sandstone structure this time consisting of thirteen arches crosses a wide valley over the Glaisnock Water. The viaduct reaching 75 feet as it crosses the river is known locally as the Diel Stane Viaduct due to a large round boulder which stood near it. If someone was to run around it then Auld Nick would appear! Here the former railway had been relegated to providing a footpath for the people of Cumnock to crossover, complete with street lamps to light the way. At least this stretch of the former railway had found an alternative use which is no than can be said for much of the rest.

At the far end of the viaduct was another housing estate and Barshare farm and also the continuation of the route towards Muirkirk. We left that for another day. While the section as we approached Cumnock had been disappointing the rest of this branchline had been in surprisingly good shape with several important viaducts. The line was closed to passengers in 1951 and to goods in 1964. Construction cannot have been cheap but King Coal was a valuable ally to releasing funds. It is a tribute to the skill of the bridge builders that their work remained in fine condition long after the coal mines which gave rise to the line's existence had been exhausted.

Glaisnock Viaduct

Main features:

C1 **Annbank Junction and Station**: 404 248 A large coal bing which sat in the 'vee' of the junction has been much reduced in size changing the scene from thirty years ago. Both lines are now single track.

C2 **Enterkine Viaduct:** 417 230 Crosses the River Ayr. Built on tall piers, the viaduct is best seen from the road bridge on the nearby B742.

C3 **Trabboch Station:** 434 218 The station was situated south of the road bridge over the railway. Nothing remains of it. Nearby coal bings give the reason for its existence. The nearby loch was created by subsidence. When the mines closed the miners were moved to Drongan.

C4 **Drongan Station:** 446 190 Now a private residence.

C5 **Belston Junction:** 481 176 Very isolated

C6 **Burnock Water Viaduct:** 504 187 A fine viaduct in good condition

C7 **Ochiltree Station:** 510 190 Now a private residence. Like all the stations between here and Cumnock, Ochiltree Station had a single platform.

C8 **Skares Station:** 529 190 New houses are being built on the site.

C9 **Ward Burn Viaduct:** 534 190 Crosses over a road and the burn.

C10 **Dumfries House Station:** 539 192 The Adam brothers built Dumfries House which lies half a mile to the north on the other side of the A70.

C11 **Glaisnock Viaduct:** 574 195 Excellent views over Cumnock. The 1895 Ordnance Survey map shows a station called Shankston Station and no Cumnock Station. *(I don't know if this was an earlier name for the Cumnock Station.)* Nearby was the Shankston Ironstone Pit.

Rankinston Branch:

C12 **Holehouse Junction.** 407 136 reached from the nearby A713 by the road to Holehouse Farm which passes under the railway.

C13 **Cairntable Halt:** 432 141 The scene has been transformed. Nothing remains.

C14 **Rankinston Station and viaduct:** 452 145 The viaduct forms part of a local walk. There are no remains of the station.

Journey D

The Lines Towards Muirkirk

The Ayr and Cumnock and the Muirkirk Branches

Nun's Cross

Two lines headed east towards Muirkirk. One started at Auchinleck, known as the Muirkirk Branch and was opened in 1848. The other opened almost a quarter of a century later and was the final part of the Ayr and Cumnock Line. Both lines converged at Cronberry Junction, on Airds Moss, once the scene of much mining activity now a lonely hamlet and then headed towards Muirkirk. The Auchinleck to Muirkirk Line closed for passengers in 1950 and the A&C Line followed in 1951.The tracks were lifted in 1964. Both walks are of about equal length (three miles) and contain many interesting features. From Cronberry Junction to Muirkirk is seven miles.

Auchinleck to Cronberry Junction

Auchinleck has changed since the turn of the century. Then, it was a mining village and a fairly important railway junction. The main line from Glasgow to Dumfries passed through the village as it still does, but the other railway connections have been severed. The station, however, closed for many years has been reopened since 1984. Gone are the mineral lines to local pits and the branch line to Muirkirk which we intended to walk as far as Cronberry Junction.

The existing railway is readily found as it crosses the main street diagonally on a rail bridge. Following the rail route leads you along a minor road heading east, sign-posted for a camp site. A modern concrete bridge crosses the railway and to the north there is a patch of waste land bordered by a housing estate. The road continues over a stone bridge with rusting side panels which was the start of our journey. The wasteland was the site of Muirkirk Junction where the Muirkirk Branch left the main line and a few yards to the left a mineral line to Gilmilnscroft Colliery had headed due north. There are no signs of the mineral line for a few miles. the first section being lost to council houses.

The Muirkirk Branch emerged from the infilled rusting bridge and headed east in a deep cutting behind the Auchinleck Social Club. The route was overgrown and strewn with rubbish. There are compensating views, however, to the south where the main line headed away on a high embankment and to the west the winding frame for one of the shafts at the former Highhouse Colliery is visible.

The line skirted fields and passed south of Fore Rogerton Farm where an unusual obstacle of discarded street lamps had to be surmounted. A wide cutting was then reached, with stratified rock faces, and beyond that. the line crossed over the Aucbinleck Burn high on an embankment. In all directions coal bings could be seen, some covered in patchy growth. From many angles there were signs of long lost mineral railways approaching the trackbed we walked.

A gate blocked the line but once climbed there was a stretch of railway which had to be carefully studied to yield its layout. An isolated section of embankment headed north-east, a large tree growing on it. This line which once led to Commondyke Pit had crossed over a minor road. Only the far abutment remained of the bridge which carried the line. Once over the road and to the west side of the track stood a tall red sandstone cross. While the writing on it was faded, eroded by the years a message could just be read. It stated that:

"At a distance of eight feet in front of this spot, the Rev Sister Laurienne was accidentally killed on the 8th August 1888"

The sister, it is believed, was from St Patrick's church and convent school which once lay a few hundred yards to the west and was searching for a lost pupil. It was as if she was enacting a modern version of the parable of the lost sheep. She was struck by a steam train, driven by a driver called Goodfellow, an unfortunate name, who happened to be a staunch Presbyterian. I found it difficult to imagine how the sister could not have heard the train coming although she had been very ill and had just returned to duties. Much ill-feeling was aroused by her death and the driver lived in fear of his life for several months until the incident was forgotten, such are the religious sensitivities in these areas.

We retraced our steps and then continued along the Muirkirk Branch. There was another coal bing to the right of the track as we entered into Birnieknowe Glen. To our left was a minor road which just ahead swung over the disused track. At the road bridge was the site of Commondyke Station. At one time there were miners' rows to either side of the bridge forming a small isolated community supplying miners to the many local pits. To the left of the former line was a crumbling brick platform which was all that remained of the station. Some old wrecked cars had been dumped at the site adding to a sense of desolation.

Once through the bridge, the route passed along a wide shallow cutting, its borders lined with trees. We were now reaching Airds Moss. To the east and north there were many signs of old mines and also opencast mining. The view was difficult to describe but words like 'lunar' and 'landscape' sprang to mind. The countryside looked horribly scarred but reassuringly, where before there had been an opencast mine near Common Farm to the north, reclamation work had improved the site. To the south was the remains of a forest planted around and over the site of Lugar Iron Works. Indeed the track became a forestry track until it reached the site of Lugar Station.

Like so many stations, Lugar was built a fair distance from the village with people from Lugar having to walk about half-a-mile to reach the station. The branch line which ran to the south of the village (on the Ayr to Cronberry line) would have been a more suitable site for a station but that line was not opened until almost a quarter of a century later. Stations meant prestige and convenience. even if the people of Lugar had known about the A&C line opening they wouldn't have wanted to wait so long. A railway did run from the station towards Lugar but it was a mineral line which branched into multiple sidings at the Lugar Iron Works built on a plateau above the village. Reclamation has removed much of the iron works but many of the administrative buildings remain.

Beyond the station site there was a bridge over a mineral line which headed north towards a now closed mine. A spur from this line joined the mainline. A broad embankment suggested multiple sidings. To the north side of the embankment there was a lily covered loch and beyond that opencast mining operations. To the south side of the embankment trapped between another bing and the former railway flowed a stream.

The embankment in turn led to a deep cutting. At the far end was an unusual brick built signal box with a curved concrete roof. It sat at the junction of the Muirkirk line with another mineral line. Keeping to the mainline we reached a three arched bridge, one arch of which crossed the road which lead to Cronberry. The final stretch of the old railway led towards Cronberry Junction and Cronberry Station.

The concentration of coal mines and iron works must have made this section of the Muirkirk Branch very busy, thronged with coal wagons being shunted or being moved to the coast, or inland towards Lanark or even south via Cumnock. The raw materials needed for the industrial revolution were here in abundance as the earth and its resources were stripped, exploited to feed the growing appetite for fuel and metals. Sadly when there was no more need the area was left to begin a painful task of reclamation, to recover from the ravages of the past.

Cumnock (A&C) to Cronberry Junction

Glaisnock Viaduct, one of two large viaducts in Cumnock was where we started our walk along the disused Ayr and Cumnock line, just east of the site of where Cumnock (A&C) Station had stood, heading towards Muirkirk. An embankment took the line away from the Glaisnock Viaduct, skirting Barshare housing estate and providing panoramic views over Cumnock.

The second bridge over the old railway on our walk still carried the Glasgow to Dumfries railway line. This line cut across the route we were walking at right angles to it. Cumnock (Old) Station, now closed, on the Glasgow to Dumfries had been situated a short distance north of this point. Where this line entered Cumnock from the north was the site of the second large thirteen arch viaduct in Cumnock, known as the Bank Viaduct. Taller than the Glaisnock viaduct by a hundred feet it was 175 feet tall as it crossed the Lugar Water.

Once passed the railway bridge, a disused spur from the mainline quickly merged with the old A&C line just before Logan where the route passed south of the sixties built housing estate. Here the route was overgrown and strewn with rubbish. However, we soon entered a long narrow, deep cutting which took us away from Logan towards Lugar. From the embankment here we could look across a deep valley containing the village, to the far side of the narrow valley where on a plateau was the site of the Lugar Iron Works. These buildings stood on a site which had a long industrial past starting as an iron and steel works then being used by the coal board. The ironworks had closed in 1928 and had been taken over by the National Coal Board until 1960 when the council occupied much of the site.

The embankment lead to a seven arched greystone viaduct over the Glenmuir Water just south of where it merges with the Bellow Water. Unfortunately the viaduct is blocked off. A glance tells you why, with the side walls crumbling and in a bad state. We had to make a detour through Lugar itself, worthy of a visit due to its industrial heritage. Indeed William Murdoch considered to be the father of the British gas industry and who worked beside James Watt, helping to pioneer steam locomotion, produced the first coal gas here. This small village had not just supplied resources for the industrial revolution but also provided some of its most important ideas. Lugar was a source of great wealth to both the G&SW and to the Baird family with its coal and pig iron production.

As we left the village, we walked up the hill out of the Lugar valley. Road realignment had removed much trace of the line. The route taken by the railway line, however, emerged from a cutting on the right on the opposite side of the road from a plaque commemorating the Rev David Houston's rescue from the Dragoon Guards in 1688. Further links to the covenanting history of this area were to emerge as we continued our walk. On the north side of the road, part of the old road could be found leading to where there once had been a road bridge over the railway. From here the route passed through a cutting towards another infilled road bridge.

The view now opened out revealing an area dominated by signs of old mine workings. We could see on a hill top overlooking the small village of Cronberry, now a short distance away, an opencast mine, the giant diggers rising like dinosaurs on the horizon scraping the coal from the surface. The Cronberry to Auchinleck railway route could be seen passing between a farmer's fields and the opencast mine.

Cronberry Junction to Muirkirk

Cronberry had once been an important railway junction with strong mining traditions but was now much reduced in size as the railways, ironstone pits and the deep mines closed. Now it is a hamlet consisting of a row of houses which have been redeveloped. It remains a bleak spot high on the Airds Moss. From here trains could have been directed to Cumnock along the A&C line, to Auchinleck or to Muirkirk. There were also signs of mineral lines from old mines feeding into the junction. Behind the site of the station traces of sidings could be seen along with an empty brick building probably used by railway workers. Nothing of the station which had been wooden existed. The site of the station was separated from the A70 by a couple of small coal bings. On the south side of the A70 stood school buildings, suggesting a once greater population.

Leaving the old station we passed by a large farm and headed out over the moor. From here to Muirkirk the line had been double track. We passed the junction for the Gasswater Branch which headed towards the road where the road bridge over this branch had been infilled. This branch was named after the Gasswater Burn and led to a barytes mine where barium sulphate was extracted.

Further on just north of Welltrees Farm at the bridge over the Bellow Water a train was derailed in 1867 crashing into the stream. Two people were killed. It would seem that it was a deliberate act by persons unknown. They certainly chose their spot carefully this section being so remote from any town that help would be slow in arriving.

Other than the noise of the traffic from the nearby road all was quiet apart from the bleating of a few sheep or the shrill call of a bird circling overhead. The route raised a few feet above the moss was in good condition with few obstacles, like missing bridges. Few trees grew anywhere and criss-crossing the moss ran poles carrying electricity to distant farms. Beside the track to the north ran a stream. A few disused brick buildings were built beside the railway, they once had contained stoves to provide shelter and warmth for railway workers who in winter must have faced difficult conditions.

As we approached the site where the A70 had crossed over the railway we saw a few hundred yards to the north a covenanting memorial where Richard Cameron and eight others were killed in a fight with dragoons in 1680. We continued our journey where the railway emerged from under the A70. There was evidence of more railway buildings and signs of more coal workings. We climbed an old coal bing to look down into the valley. There was a marked difference from the bleak moorland we had left. The view we saw was more attractive. To the east there were a few small woods and a larger one which blocked our sight of Muirkirk and in the distance was Cairn Table rising to over 1300 feet. To the south stood bleak hills but the railway fortunately headed due east.

The route taken by the disused railway still ran parallel to the road but further away from it. Between the two, ran the River Ayr on its journey to the coast from its source near Glenbuck. We passed former railway workers cottages and then passed under a wooden bridge which appeared none too safe. An abandoned railway track from another closed mine ran alongside the line on which we travelled. The railway route now approached the large wood we had seen from a distance, keeping just to the south end of it on an embankment. There were glimpses through the trees of Smallburn the housing estate on the outskirts of Muirkirk, and also of the tower of the

Kames Centre which was where Muirkirk Station had been located. Leaving the woods behind, we encountered the site of a missing bridge over a minor road quickly followed by another over a burn. It was easy to cross both obstacles though in winter the burn might pose more problems. The missing bridge had been known as '21' (it was bridge number 21) and a pool next to it had been used by youths for swimming. Further upstream there was a memorial cairn to John Loudon McAdam inventor of the tar macadam road process who came from Ayr. His involvement at Muirkirk had been an attempt to extract tar from tar pits, a venture which failed.

The disused route then entered a cutting which ran next to Muirkirk golf course. The par four, fifth hole looked inviting but we pushed on towards the station site.

Not much remained to link the station site to the railway. We first reached the site of the sidings and engine sheds where a go-kart track had been built. Rows of miners and railwaymens' cottages and the once substantial engine sheds had all been removed. This had been the site of the first Muirkirk Station which had been replaced by a newer station in 1896 beyond the road. Ironically more of the older station remained in existence with part of the platform and the station building still standing. The tower of the Kames Centre with its large clock faces stopped for many a year and now used as an adult learning centre lay to our right.

Muirkirk for many years was the sole producer of iron in Ayrshire and with gas lighting being introduced in its iron works before any other factory in Scotland, the production could go on all day. Before the railway age there had even been a canal built to exploit the resources offered by this area. The iron works closed in 1923 and Muirkirk's importance as a railway centre started to decline.

To the east of the engine sheds beyond Furnace Road was where the main station buildings were located after 1896, along with a brick built signal box. On the approach to the station there had been a footbridge brought from Darvel after a young girl had been killed crossing at, what was then, a level crossing. Passenger trains to the west had stopped in 1950 but a service to Lanark had persisted until 1964. A dog food factory making dog meal then occupied the site and evidence of loading ramps for trucks still persisted but the scene was one of dereliction.

Iron production and coal explained why railway companies were keen to reach here. Muirkirk was the meeting point of the Glasgow and South Western Railway and the Caledonian Railway bitter rivals as we will discover in the railway walk from Muirkirk to Coalburn. This was where east met west in terms of the two railways.

Turning away from the station site we walked along Furnace Road towards Muirkirk a distance of about half-a-mile. To the east of the road once lay the iron works as the name suggests. To the other side of the road where there had been gas works, there was now a quarry. High on the hill above Muirkirk to the north, diggers could be seen stripping coal from the ground from a new opencast mine. Muirkirk's past still lingers but the railway no longer plays a part in it.

Signal box near to Cronberry Junction

Main features:

D1 **Auchinleck:** 558 218 Start of the walk
D2 **Nun's Cross:** 577 223 Beware of the bull!
D3 **Commondyke Station:** 578 222
D4 **Lugar Station:** 590 222 Nothing remains.
D5 **Bellow Water Viaduct:** 602 224 The brick built signal box can be seen to the west of the viaduct.
D6 **Cronberry Station:** 608 226 The nearby school buildings have been converted into an Indian and European restaurant. Worth noting!
D7 **Glaisnock Viaduct:** 574 195 Starting point for the walk from Cumnock to Cronberry Junction.
D8 **Glenmuir Water Viaduct:** 559 214 Closed off - you have to detour
D9 **Gasswater Branch:** 612 230 The mines are on the other side of the A70. Great care required near the mine!
D10 **Covenanting Memorial.** 643 259 There is a path to it from the A70.
D11 **Muirkirk Station:** 698 267 To the east of Furnace Road.

Journey E

Linespotting

A Journey To Glenbuck On The Line With No Trains

Auldhouseburn Viaduct

One railway line in the Muirkirk area had a most unusual history for the simple reason that no train ever ran on it. (Although some sources claim that one train inspecting the line did travel on it.) The Mid Lanark, Spireslack and Muirkirk line as it was called ran from Spireslack near Glenbuck to Muirkirk. It was an extension of the Caledonian Railway's Glenbuck Branch which ran from Coalburn in Lanarkshire to the hills behind Glenbuck.

The Glenbuck Branch existed to remove the coal from the mines in the Glenbuck area. The 'new line' as the people of Glenbuck called it, was to take the CR right into the G&SW heartland of Ayrshire with the aim of challenging that company's monopoly of coal transportation in the area. The G&SW was under pressure not just from the CR but also from mine owners in Ayrshire to reduce costs for carrying coal. The CR which already had a line which ran to Muirkirk from Lanark via Douglas was a welcome intruder to encourage competition. Indeed an act promoting an alternative railway line through Ayrshire supported by Ayrshire mine owners was passed by parliament but did not receive assent due to an election. Eventually, to beat off the opposition the G&SW was forced to cut costs and when the act failed they thought that they had held back the Caley. However a further Act of Parliament in 1896 gave permission for the CR to build the extension from near Glenbuck along with other lines in Lanarkshire, but with a sting in the tail. When all the railways were completed the G&SW would also get running rights over the extension. Now the boot was on the other foot and it was the CR who were now under threat themselves as the G&SW Railway could now look at developing business in the lucrative Douglas coalfield. Hence some claim why the railway was never opened, even although it was constructed and the track laid at considerable expense. The line was officially abandoned in 1910. Others give different reasons. Some claim that geological faults in the coalfields near Glenbuck meant that the mines there were never developed: others that a fault in the Auldhouseburn Viaduct near Muirkirk meant that the line could never open.

Interested to find what remained of this line we headed east from the site of Muirkirk Station. Almost immediately, there was evidence of several disused tracks as we entered woods a few hundred yards from the station site. A coal bing covered the site of an old sand pit where Auldhouseburn coal pit, which closed in 1911, had been. Two lines passed either side of the bing almost converging on the far side where they headed east in parallel. On each track there were two missing bridges crossing over minor roads. The track nearer to Muirkirk was called Baird's line and reached as far as Glenbuck. Baird's railway was built by the Baird Iron & Coal Company. The track on which we walked was the main CR line east to Lanark opened in 1874 and closed in 1964. On the CR line there were two additional intact bridges passing over what looked like a dried up stream. A short walk along the track past Crossflats Farm brought us to the remains of Auldhouseburn Viaduct which crossed the meandering River Ayr.

We had followed the old CR line. The line we wanted to follow, the Mid Lanark, Spireslack and Muirkirk Line had branched at this point crossing over the now demolished viaduct. Ahead lay a four mile walk at a gradient of 1 in 50 crossing three major viaducts.

The brick base of a signal box built to control the junction and which was never used remained covered in nettles. Beside the base of the signal box was a strong retaining wall supporting the CR line as it headed east, We clambered down towards the viaduct and noticed a double lined brick tunnel underneath the start of the viaduct. There was a dry ditch which ran though the tunnel and extended both sides. It was a continuation of the ditch we had seen earlier. What we had discovered was the remains of a mile long canal built in 1789 linking the furnaces at Muirkirk to coal and limestone deposits at Lightshaw and Auldhouseburn. We spent some times following the line of the old canal which ran between the CR line and the Baird line. We now realised why they were additional bridges on the CR line. They took the CR line over the canal. However walking old canal routes, even dry ones did not appeal so we returned to the viaduct.

Baird's Railway passed under the first arch of the Auldhouseburn Viaduct which had now collapsed. The CR and Baird's lines could be seen often running in parallel lying to the south of the River Ayr until near Glenbuck.

Thick stone walls supported the Spireslack line at the start of the viaduct. The Auldhouseburn viaduct had been blown up in 1942, providing demolition practice for the army by letting the sappers practice on real structures. They needed the practice because the first pier admittedly twice the thickness of the other piers still stood, the masonry at the top splayed outwards, but still intact. Beyond that, stood one more pier before the river. On the other side of the river which was easily crossed (there is a nearby road for wetter days) a line of six demolished piers had stood, all now a pile of crumpled masonry. It looked as if the sapper had perfected his skill as he reached the far end of the viaduct. The final support for the viaduct stood on high ground known as Torhill next to the A70.The Auldhouseburn Viaduct was no cheap effort but had been a substantial structure. Who would pay the costs incurred if they never intended to use it?

Within a few yards of the viaduct was the rail bridge over the A70. Now only the abutments remained. The next stretch lay high on an embankment towards Lightshaw Farm an area which had once had several working mines closed early this century, but of which there was now little evidence. The line was well preserved, sheep grazing on its banks. At the farm we were forced to detour or face having to cross a garden. We took the detour joining the line at the site of another missing bridge. Ahead was a further stretch of embankment. Looking south across the valley there was a standing stone in the field next to the disused railway. A local story says it was cast there by the devil from the nearby Cairn Table hill when he spotted John Brown, a local covenantor, praying in the field. The stone is made of basalt not normally found in the area.

We reached a further missing bridge. Today you would have speculated that the bridge was built to allow the local farmer access between two fields. However that was not the situation in the past when a tramway from Lightshaw Pits to the north passed under the bridge and headed towards the A70 and the River Ayr. Two bridges carried the tramway over the river to a network of sidings from where the coal was carried along Balrd's line to the furnaces at Muirkirk. Across the valley the CR line and the Baird line could be seen running beside each other and between them was the canal. At one time the canal had been the means of transport and it extended as far as this point. If the Spireslack Branch, had opened presumably a spur would have been built from it to connect with the Lightshaw Pits. Situated to the east of the tramway as it crossed the river was Waukmill, a disused flax mill. Little of the mill remains today.

At this point, there were three lines, including the line we were walking, travelling east. Soon there would only be two. Ahead was a cutting and beyond that the first signs of an opencast coalfield. At the other end of the cutting we found a fence marking the edge of the coalfield. Our route was blocked. Apart from one isolated section of embankment there was no further sign of the railway. We climbed out of the cutting towards two tall stones on a nearby hilltop and surveyed the scene. To the west was Muirkirk. To the east was a large working coalfield. On my 1989 edition of the Ordnance Survey map the coalfield had lain to the north of the line. Now it lay to the east and south. As the original coalfield had been developed the route of the railway which should have turned north-east at this point had been destroyed. Keeping to the north of the boundary fence and on what was now reclaimed land we headed towards the valley of the Ponesk Burn to see if anything remained of the viaduct over it. Reaching the deep and narrow valley we searched north. On the far side of the burn was a coal mine. Stones and rubble from that mine had spilled down the far side of the valley almost covering a demolished pier of the viaduct. Little remained apart from a pile of bricks where another pier had stood. Looking across at the mine we saw the abutments of a bridge over the railway. The railway track should have been passing through a coniferous wood according to our map but the quarry and opencast operations were steadily eating into the trees. On the other side of the narrow fringe of trees that still stood, there was a giant quarry where there once was a large wood and the railway.

There was nothing else to do but walk back to the A70. We indulged in line hopping and crossed over the River Ayr to the other CR line and continued east. While there was a large gap in the line it had not been totally removed as we discovered when we reached Glenbuck. However anyone attempting the journey would be advised to leave the Spireslack Line after Lightshaw Farm until they reached Glenbuck. **Opencast mines are dangerous - keep well away!**

Glenbuck, a village noted for its famous football team, the Glenbuck Cherrypickers, and the famous Shankly brothers is now a village under attack. From the west the opencast operations creep ever closer to the village. There was a loop road through the village before it was straightened out, bypassing Glenbuck. The west side of the loop road has now been claimed by the ever encroaching mining operation. The old CR route can be seen running beside the straightened main road. Gone also was any evidence of the station, which was near to the minor road to Darnhunch Farm and was on the CR line. A path used to lead from the village to the station. Beside the path was a large stone embedded in the ground with peculiar 'hair-pin' marks on it. It was claimed in local folk-lore that they were made when a young woman was killed by her husband who hit her with a stone so hard that the imprint of her 'hair-pin' was left on the stone!

To the east of Glenbuck is a loch which the railway crossed on a causeway as it entered Lanarkshire. Here is the source of the River Ayr. The loch was created to supply water to the mills at Catrine. Trees and a farm shield what remains of Glenbuck from passing traffic. Following the narrow twisting road towards the village we found a row of derelict cottages and no sign of the famous football park. Iron furnaces opened soon after those at Muirkirk and coal mines had kept this village alive.

To the west, the opencast operations towered. To the north-west stood the coniferous woods and beside them stood the piers of the third and final viaduct on the Spireslack railway, the Glenbuck Viaduct over the Stottencleugh Burn. The railway had returned.

We walked towards the viaduct past Spireslack farm. The area to our left bore the scars of the Grasshill pits closed in 1933. With the closure of these pits the drift away from the village began as miners looked for other work, many moving to Muirkirk. The viaduct had three piers, the central one I estimated at 75 feet. Stacked against the central pier were rusting hutches or tubs used to bring the coal out of the mines. After a steep climb we reached the top of the east bank of the valley of the burn. One final missing bridge and then we were in a deep cutting which blocked any view of Glenbuck. The route was remarkably well-preserved as it edged towards the Douglas Moor. Once passed the cutting, a bleak valley greeted us. High on the hills to the north was the beginning of a wood which marked the boundary between Ayrshire and Lanarkshire(now South Lanarkshire). Signs of other former lines appeared as we reached the site of Spireslack Coal Pit closed for almost a century. The Galawhistle Burn flowed from the north under the disused route giving its name to the junction which lay ahead where the old mineral line from Galawhistle Pit joined the railway from the south. This had been the starting point for the Mid Lanark, Spireslack and Muirkirk Line and the county of Lanark.

Perched on the nearby Hagshaw hill were a group of twenty-six wind-turbines, propeller blades slowly, silently rotating at the top of steel shafts trapping even more of the resources from the area, this time at little cost to the residents. It seemed as if Glenbuck was always destined to be exploited for its resources.

We headed back towards Glenbuck using the disused Galawhistle Line which led through more desolate scenes of old discarded mine workings and deep quarries eventually reaching a road above the village. Despite the bleak scenes there was definitely an atmosphere pervading the environment, a brooding sense of the past. I had a growing sense of admiration for those who laboured and sweated to extract at a terrible cost, precious resources from these hills. Distant battles between the Caley and the Sou' West seemed an irrelevance, the new battle was for the life of Glenbuck itself under threat from a fresh expansion of the opencast field to the west. I could well understand how these hills had helped fashion men of iron like Bill Shankly, the former Liverpool manager. You would have had to be strong to survive.

There was a loud peal of thunder from the direction of Cairn Table and a flash of lightning lit up the valley. Perhaps 'the deil' was coming looking for John Brown again. It seemed a good time to stop our journey!

Main features.

E1 **Auldhouseburn Viaduct:** 708 277 With the remains of the viaduct, canal, the base of an old signal box, the CR line and Baird's line the area is worth a visit.

E2 **Ponesk Viaduct:** 731 294 Probably not worth visiting. The brick piers lie collapsed in the valley.

E3 **Glenbuck Viaduct**: 744 300 The piers remain.

E4 **Glenbuck:** 750 295 A must for Liverpool fans paying homage to Bill Shankly. Slowly being squeezed out of existence by the encroaching opencast mine. There are no remains of the station left. There is an interesting causeway across Glenbuck Loch used by the railway for its journey further east.

Journey F

The Catrine Branch

A tale of cotton and explosives

The Catrine Branch carried passengers for only forty years although it may have been used for a few years after for the occasional Sunday School trip. Goods traffic persisted, however, for many years after the closure of the line to passengers on the 3rd May 1943. Opened on the 1st September 1903 it allowed the G&SW railway direct access to the James Finlay cotton mills at Catrlne. As well as moving goods the railway encouraged people to visit the famous mills to view their couple of harnessed fifty foot diameter wheels once the largest in the world.

Like all changes, the railway brought unexpected benefits, allowing the people of Catrine easy access to Ayr and other parts. The branch left the main Glasgow to Dumfries railway just north of Brackenhill Farm which gave its name to the junction. Sweeping round a low hill it was soon in sight of the busy A76 trunk road which it passed under. While the junction with the old railway is fenced off and trees have been planted, the line of the track is clearly visible although some of the cutting approaching the road has been infilled. The only access to this part is to park in the parking place next to the road bridge over the former railway and then walk to the main line and back.

Once under the bridge, the railway continued through a deep cutting. A bridge over the line which once carried a pipe is still intact, and beyond that, there was a sandstone bridge giving farm access. The railway then emerged from the cutting heading towards Catrine, which was clearly visible ahead, on an embankment. To our left ran the B713 also heading towards Catrine, with Whiteflats farm buildings on the far side of the road.

The reason for the embankment became clear when we encountered the bricked off abutment where the bridge over the Bogend Burn began. The bridge had consisted of a fairly high sandstone pier, now standing in isolation, along with the two sandstone abutments. It was not too difficult to scramble down to the burn and the far side was easily climbed. When built, this part of the railway, just over a mile from Brackenhill Junction, was still out in the country. Now the site of the bridge backed onto a housing estate as Catrine had expanded over the years. From here, maybe not surprisingly, the condition of the track deteriorated and within a hundred yards the route was lost to roads which had been built to service a housing estate. Whiteflat Bridge over the railway still stood, indicating the direction that the railway had taken and now used by the residents of the housing estate. Everything else was lost.

The site of the station terminus, which was just beyond Whiteflat Bridge could be recognised only from old photographs because of the row of tall trees which had stood to the right of the track. Of the station, we could find nothing, the whole area now being part of an industrial estate. The station had consisted of a single long platform with sidings and a goods shed to the left.

After a promising start, any remnants of the railway had been swallowed up. This however, was the second time that the station had been dismantled. In 1909 enterprising burglars suspecting that the safe in the station contained cash, blew up the safe and most of the station, having been over generous with the explosives.

The cotton trade survived the railway closing and in 1950 a new mill was built. The new mill only remained open until 1968 and by then, the old mill had gone, destroyed by fire in 1963. The mills and the railway have both now left Catrine for good but much still remains to attract the visitor.

Main Features:

F1 **Brackenhill Junction:** 520 242 The embankment near the main line can be seen.

F2 **Bogend Burn Viaduct:** 526 253 The abutments and pier remain.

F3 **Catrine Station:** 531 257 No sign of it although the tall trees give some indication of its position.

Journey G

The Irvine Valley Branch

Hurlford to Darvel

Railway cutting near Darvel - Loudoun hill in the distance

The Irvine Valley east of Kilmarnock with its mineral wealth and the towns of Galston, Newmilns and Darvel was a fertile ground for an expanding railway network and was also another place for the G&SW and the CR to confront each other. A branch to Galston opened on 9th August 1848 and further east to Newmilns almost two years later on the 20th May 1850, but it was not until the 1st June 1896 that the railway reached Darvel. What was a branch line, became a through line when the Darvel to Strathaven line was opened on the 1st May 1905. This gave a direct route for the G&SW into Lanarkshire with the CR protecting its heartland of the Lanarkshire coalfields. Jointly run by the G&SW and the CR, this ten mile section was never successful and was finally closed in 1939 with the rails being lifted in 1951. By 1964 the rest of the line east of Kilmarnock had been closed.

Our journey began at Hurlford where the River Irvine weaves its way through the town. The main Kilmarnock to Dumfries line cut across the river high on a viaduct, just north of the site of the former Portland Iron

Works, now redeveloped, which were located between the railway and the River Irvine where it winds its way through Crookedholm. Closed by the turn of the century 'the furnaces' had an extensive rail network feeding onto the main line. Just to the south of the junction with what became the Darvel Branch, the Moss Sidings branched south-west from the mainline. The sidings had been removed by the turn of the century.

To many the beating heart of the G&SW network was the engine shed at Hurlford, where the company's locomotive works were located at the start of the branch line to Darvel. Moved a couple of miles from Kilmarnock where there was no room for further expansion of the engine sheds there, a village grew up around the works in Hurlford. Houses for workers known as 'the blocks' were built next to the engine sheds and there even was a school, hall, church and shop. Hurlford was in a good position being located next to the junction where the railway along the Irvine Valley branched from the main line south to Dumfries. Hurlford itself had a station on the main line and there was a halt at Barleith for the Darvel branch. Mineral sidings were also provided, often occupied by coal wagons from the numerous surrounding pits with much of the coal destined for export from Troon Harbour. With the end of steam and with Ayr being better located to meet the needs of the remaining coal pits the engine shed at Hurlford was no longer needed and was closed on the 3rd October 1966. The sheds, the sidings and the station were removed and the site is now occupied by the Johnnie Walker distillery (United Distillers), which have their own sidings, so that the railway connection is not totally lost.

From the distillery the line headed east on a long straight section, running alongside a housing estate. Ahead could be seen in the distance Loudounhill, the unique shape of its volcanic neck indicating the direction we were going to walk. Within a few hundred yards was Mayfield Junction where the Gatehead and Hurlford Line joined the Darvel Line.

The Gatehead and Hurlford Line branched from Bellfield Junction, near Kilmarnock and passed under the Dumfries line and to the south of the engine sheds at Hurlford before joining up with the Darvel Line. With the opening of the Darvel to Strathaven Line it was hoped that this line would take coal traffic from the Lanarkshire coalfields to Troon Harbour and save congestion at Kilmarnock. This traffic never materialised and what was probably an attempt by the G&SW to win work from the CR failed. Heading north from this junction was the Mayfield Branch a mineral line serving among other pits the Loudoun Collieries to the north of Galston on the far side of the River Irvine. To complete a busy site the Portland

Coal Pits Nos 6 and 7, located to the south of the line, fed into the network here. In a scene, suitable for 'past and present' photographs all that remains are the trackbeds of the Darvel and Mayfield branches now used as a path for dog walking.

The route continued over the three arch viaduct over the Cessnock Water towards a road bridge. To the right were more pits, this time the Portland Pits Nos 5 and 8 and again all traces have been removed. Just before the bridge to the side were some abandoned concrete sleepers and at the bridge the local farmer had built a metal barrier so that the arch could be used as a shelter for his animals. Ahead the first houses in Galston could be seen and along the direction we had walked houses in Hurlford were also visible. A feature of this journey along the Irvine Valley was that the walker was never far from a town.

Through a short cutting were more signs of this area's coal mining past. An crumbling embankment headed towards Holmes Pithead No4 which lay to the north of the line, with some remains of the pithead visible.

Galston was now getting closer with Barward Farm and the site of what had been the next bridge over the line which led to the farm. Steps now led up to the infilled road bridge and back down to the track on the far side where a mineral railway headed north to Goatfoot Colliery, and where Gauchalland Colliery No2 was situated with a quarry to the south of the track now occupied by a road depot. Other pits were located to the south of the line. Most of the mines had closed by the mid 1930s and by the time of nationalisation in 1947, the coal industry in the Irvine Valley, once so prosperous was finished.

Entering Galston the A71 is crossed and the route continued until the breeze block wall of a haulage contractor blocked the way. If that does not sound attractive then ahead was the red bricked dome of the St Sophia's R.C. Church and the towering Barr Castle, with its connections to John Knox. Truly an ecumenical scene! The yard is by-passed by a small bridge and path leading between the yard and a school. Ahead now there is a road bridge over a burn. If the first road to the right is taken once the bridge is crossed, the route taken by the railway is picked up again at Carnalea Court. A scramble up the embankment, where the stone outlines of the former road bridge can still be seen embedded in the side of the embankment, to Station Road and then down a cul-de-sac on the other side, brings you to the site of the former station in Galston now occupied by housing and a BT telephone exchange. The station, once very busy, had a booking office and sidings to one side and a waiting room on the other platform. There was also a footbridge. Due to subsidence caused by mine-workings the station offices were at an angle to the platform.

A walk along Belvedere Road, turning left at Cairn View takes you through Galston.

On the other side of the valley is Loudoun Castle and to the right the adventure park, one of the Castle's many attractions. surrounded by a wood.

Beyond the housing estate was a stretch of embankment where the Maxwood Colliery, sidings and miners' rows were located. There were several other mines in this area. The disused trackbed is high above the A71 at this point. Between the disused track and the road was the River Irvine and beside the river was Barr Mill, a corn mill now a ruin and further east Strath Mill which was a paper mill. possibly dating back to 1639, now demolished. Near Strath Mill was the start of a long deep cutting. On the other side of the road is Loudoun Golf Course, a fire station and a school which are seen at times from the trackbed when the view is not blocked by the steep side of the cutting.

On entering Newmilns, there were bleaching works to the left at Lanfine. On the approach to the former station site, the route is blocked by a shed. Cutting down the embankment to Stoneygate Road provides a lesson in the other main industry of the Irvine Valley - lace. The site of the railway station in Newmilns is occupied by an industrial estate. Whose main occupant is the Vesuvius Crucible Company. This is the first time that I've known a station to be taken over by a volcano! The station buildings, platforms and signal box have been removed along with any sign of the 'Bogey Line', a continuous chain which carried coal from the drift mine near Windyhill Farm just to the south.

The route taken by the railway, beyond the station, is rediscovered as you turn right and walk along Browns Road. On the right hand side of the trackbed is a massive retaining wall, built to hold back the hillside at Mount Pleasant Farm. The opening of the railway to Darvel was delayed, until on the third attempt the wall was considered safe. Parts of the wall are thirty feet thick and the wall is thirty-four feet high. However that wasn't the only major railway engineering works in Newmilns because beyond what are now the abutments of the railway bridge over a road and a short stretch of embankment, is a 26 arch viaduct which dominates this part of Newmilns. The second arch crosses the River Irvine, while many of the other arches are occupied by small businesses. While it is once again disappointing that there is no access to the viaduct, walking beside it allows you to appreciate the size of the construction and the narrowness of the Irvine Valley at Newmilns which forced the railway builders to take this route, which still involved re-routing the road to Darvel.

At the far end of the viaduct the next destination of the Irvine Valley railway can be seen - Darvel and beyond the town, the familiar shape of Loudounhill. The river now flows on the right hand side of the railway, the railway having crossed over the River Irvine in Newmilns. To the left and up a steep slope is the main road. The road bridge over the former railway is soon reached. where the road cuts down towards Darvel. Now filled in, it does not provide an obstacle on the final stretch. With mainly housing to the north and factories to the south the railway cut through Darvel. A final missing bridge and then the empty site of Darvel Station was reached, hemmed in by textile factories. The station site was extensive with the station and its platforms to the north of the site and a goods yard and sidings, along with a turntable to the south. At the eastern end of the site, there is still part of the approach road to the station, otherwise all signs have been removed. The station which was long fought for by the residents of the town, lasted only sixty-eight years. Once busy bringing lace workers from east and west, the station was hardly used in later years and was closed in 1965.

So ended an interesting eight mile walk through the Irvine Valley. Still noted for its textile works, Darvel is probably most famous as the birthplace of Alexander Fleming, whose discovery of penicillin revolutionised the world of medicine and whose memorial is located in the main street next to the cenotaph.

The railway of course continued on towards Loudounhill, (historic site of a battle where Robert Bruce defeated the English in 1307), re-crossing the River Irvine on a thirteen arch viaduct which was demolished in 1986 but Darvel was the final destination for today. The ten miles to Strathaven along the next section of the disused railway could be left to another day.

Newmilns Viaduct

Main Features:

G1 **Hurlford Station:** 449 367 Was located on main line just south of A71. Houses built on site. Still a signal box near the former station site.

G2 **Barleith Station:** 456 361 Now part of United Distilleries (Johnnie Walker) site

G3 **Mayfield Junction:** 461 361 Use your imagination!

G4 **Galston Station:** 504 364 Part of a modern housing development. Nearby Loudoun Castle is worth a visit.

G5 **Newmilns Station:** 533 370 Occupied by an industrial estate.

G6 **Newmilns Viaduct:** 536 372 Not very high, but very long and divides this area of the town, known as the Green.

G7 **Darvel Station:** 563 377 Desolate site.

Journey H

Cross-Country Lines West of Kilmarnock

The Kilmarnock to Dalry Branch and the Busby Branch

Rainbow sculpture near site of Dreghorn Station

The Kilmarnock to Dalry Branch connected the town of Kilmarnock to the main Glasgow to Ayr Line. At Crosshouse Junction (originally named Busby Junction) there was a branch to Irvine known as the Busby Line. Both journeys begin at Crosshouse Junction.

Kilmarnock to Dalry

The people of Kilmarnock were aggrieved when the plans for the expansion of the railways in Ayrshire seemed to bypass them. The chosen route for the railway from Glasgow headed down the Garnock Valley to Irvine leaving them with the consolation of a branch line from Dalry. Not wanting to be left out they suggested an alternative route by Barrhead to Kilmarnock and then to Troon, with the stretch from Kilmarnock largely following the route of the Duke of Portland's Railway between Kilmarnock and Troon. The problem was one of gradients. The Garnock Valley route was easier to construct while the proposed Barrhead route with difficult gradients was both more expensive to construct and would have stretched to the limits the abilities of the engines at that time to cope with the route. George Stephenson, no less was called in to settle the issue and sided with the Garnock Valley route which was duly opened in 1840. The branch from Dalry was built and in operation three years later.

With the building of the route from Kilmarnock to Dumfries and the south a few years later, southbound traffic faced a long route via Dalry and Kilmarnock. Pressure again built for a more direct line and with improvements in engine design this became more feasible and after another long battle with the Caledonian Railway, who also wanted to reach Kilmarnock, a joint line called the Glasgow, Barrhead and Kilmarnock Joint Line was opened by 1873. Southbound passenger traffic now used the joint line, which was nine miles shorter, but a lot of the freight traffic still used the Kilmarnock to Dalry Branch with its easier gradients. There was also a local passenger service on the Kilmarnock to Dalry Branch. Between Kilmarnock and Dalry, on the eleven and a quarter mile route, were Crosshouse Station, originally called Busby Station where the Busby Branch departed for Irvine, Cunninghamhead Station and Montgreenan Station and for a short time Dalry Junction Station. Local passenger traffic was light with no towns along the route.

Today the route begins as a long siding at Bonnyton next to the former headquarters of Southhook Pottery. Between here and Crosshouse Junction there were sidings at Bonnyton, Woodhill to Woodhill Colliery and from Fardlehill Junction to Greenhill Colliery. The last two pits and sidings were very close to each other, although there also was another Woodhill Pit to the north of the line. The track still extends for a mile, now relegated to a long siding to Greenhill Cottages where a road bridge has been filled in blocking the track. On the far side there are still concrete sleepers a reminder of the time when this section was used for an experiment with long welded rails.

The track crossed a three arch viaduct before reaching Busby or Crosshouse Junction just before the double arched road bridge over the line to the north of Knockentiber. Busby Junction was renamed as Crosshouse Junction in 1924 when the regrouping had occurred and the route became part of the LMS area, probably to avoid confusion with the Busby Junction on the East Kilbride branch line, where that line departs from the Glasgow to Neilston line. To the east of the bridge was the junction and signal box with the branch from Busbiehead Colliery, which gave the junction its original name, reaching the main line by a cutting from the left. There were many tracks at this point serving the pits and the main railway lines. The Busby Branch and the Kilmarnock and Dalry Branch railways ran in parallel for a few yards until they passed under the double arched bridge, each line taking a different arch.

Situated just beyond the bridge was Crosshouse Station. Originally the station was opened as Busby Station In 1848 but closed in less than two years. Crosshouse Station was opened on the same site in September 1872. The puzzle is why the station was called Crosshouse and not Knockentiber. Both villages at the time the railway was built were of equal status and Knockentiber is a lot closer! Crosshouse is a small village, in recent years the site of a busy modern general hospital, one mile to the south.

Crosshouse Station was located where the Busby Branch and the Kilmarnock to Dalry line veered away from each other. A triangular platform filled the vee between the two lines. To the left was the Busby Line and to the right was the continuation of the Kilmarnock to Dalry Line. On the right hand side of the Kilmarnock line heading west were sidings which led to an engine shed and some railway cottages.

Nowadays trees press in on the station site. A wire fence with concrete posts which separated the two lines after the closure of the Busby Branch, has now rusted away. Nothing of the platforms remained. The engine shed and cottages survive as a car scrap yard. However, an angry guard dog did its job of keeping us from exploring the site.

The two lines diverged at the junction with the Dalry line on an embankment climbing above the Busby Branch. The jagged peaks of Arran lay ahead as we crossed the first bridge over a farm track. The route was very straight and with few missing bridges or other obstacles meant that the walking was easy despite some waterlogged cuttings. Enjoying the countryside and the views in all directions we took our time to cover the two and quarter miles between Crosshouse and the site of the first station on the line to open, which was originally called Stewarton, even although Stewarton was almost five miles away. On the approach to the station we could find no trace of the branch line to the south towards Warwickhill Colliery. This was the first link to a coal mine on the stretch from Crosshouse. Of the station to the east of where the B769 crossed the line by a road bridge, there was little sign. Part of a stone wall was all that remained with no signs of the two platforms or the station buildings. The station was very remote with only small villages anywhere near it. It dropped its claim to serve Stewarton on the 1st September 1873 when it changed its name to Cunninghamhead over two years after Stewarton Station (this time in Stewarton) had been opened on the Glasgow, Barrhead and Kilmarnock Joint Line. The station finally closed in 1951.

Beyond Cunninghamhead Station there was a succession of bridges over the line as the route passed through a cutting before emerging on an embankment which lead to a three arch viaduct over the valley of the Annick Water near Roddinghill Farm.

A short section beside the farm was being used as a horse jumping course but there were few other obstacles. At the end of a long shallow cutting, the views to the south and west took in the tower-blocks and church spires of Irvine, the ICI plant at Ardeer and the ever present peaks of Arran. Still we hadn't encountered a missing bridge and it wasn't until we reached the abutments of the former rail bridge over the A736 that we were forced to leave the trackbed. On the far side of the missing bridge was a further cutting with more horse jumping obstacles set out along the former route. As we approached the site of Montgreenan Station, the trackbed had been used as a dump.

Montgreenan Station was to the west of the next road bridge over the line. The garden of a nearby house had been extended over the route and on the station side of the bridge was also being used as a garden. The station buildings, although altered, still stood, with the former sidings to the north of the station buildings having become a caravan park. Between Montgreenan Station and Kilwinning which stood to the south had been a major coal mining area, served by the Doura Branch which ran through the grounds of Eglinton Castle, and linked many pits in the area feeding coal to the Eglinton Ironworks until they closed in 1924. (The Doura Branch is described more fully in Journey J.) Montgreenan Station opened on the 1st February 1878 and was closed in 1955. To the north of the station in woods stands Montgreenan House, now a restaurant.

For the first time the route taken by the line had been ploughed into the neighbouring fields but a road bridge several hundred yards ahead indicated the direction we should take. Once past the bridge and another cutting we approached the five arched Lugton Water Viaduct, the only major viaduct on the route. To the north-west the buildings for the local quarry were visible. At one time there had been a tramway from the track to the quarry.

A local farmer had built a barrier under the next road bridge but from here until we reached the abutments of the former rail bridge over the B778 the abandoned track was easy to walk. Beyond the B778 is a stretch of private land with access denied. It is in this area that the Lanarkshire and Ayrshire Line (see Journey I) crossed over the Kilmarnock to Dalry Branch by a three arched viaduct. This site can be viewed form the road as you walk towards Kilwinning. We had completed a five and a half mile section.

It is possible to pick up the abandoned track on the far side of Kilwinning by following the road to the right just before the cemetery, as you enter Kilwinning This road winds over the L&A route. giving good views of the seven-arch viaduct over the River Garnock and eventually crosses under the Kilmarnock to Dalry Branch as it heads towards Dalry Junction. At Dalry Junction, formerly known as Kilcush Junction there was a station, called Dalry Junction Station which was closed at the end of 1859. It had platforms serving both the Ayr line and the branch line. Today Dalry retains a station on the Glasgow to Ayr line. There was a lot of early railway activity in this area as Dalry was one of the first centres of iron production in Ayrshire, but the furnaces had closed by 1871. There were also many coal mines in the area but only one was working by the end of the second world war. Roche Chemical Works still use the railway and have sidings. known as Swinlees Sidings north of Dalry.

The Busby Branch
The Irvine and Crosshouse Railway

The Busby Branch, an important cross country route branching from the Kilmarnock to Dalry line west of Kilmarnock and reaching Irvine and hence the Clyde ports was a busy goods line, serving many pits and brickworks along the route. The line opened on 22nd May 1848. When the line was opened a new station was built at Dreghorn and in 1890, Springside Halt was added. At the west end of the branch the railway connected to Irvine Station and its extensive marshalling yards. Irvine Station was already open and was part of the Glasgow to Ayr route. Traffic using the branch line could easily access the Clyde ports.

Due to pits, both coal and ironstone, brickworks and quarries the line generated a lot of freight traffic. It was also used to transport explosives from the Ardeer explosives factory onto the Glasgow to Dumfries mainline at Kilmarnock. Passenger business was built up by running trains to Ardeer and by linking to the coast routes and the Clyde steamers. Many excursions from all along the Irvine Valley were run. Beeching axed the line and the last train ran in October 1965. Crosshouse Station, part of which was on the Dalry line lasted until 1969.

Despite finding the route between Busby Junction and Irvine one of the best preserved and easiest to walk for most of its length, little to connect the route to the railway remains. Landscapers have succeeded in removing most signs of the line's industrial past and only a few spoil heaps remain. This route may have changed dramatically but with a map and imagination you can be again in the heart of a rich coalfield which was a hive of railway activity.

Heading west from the site of Crosshouse Station was a path which ran along the route of the Busby Branch with metal posts concreted in at intervals across it, ensuring that nothing faster than a bike could make the journey. We left the bleakness of the station site behind passing the remains of a gravel pit situated between the two diverging lines, with the Dalry line starting to climb on an embankment. Already we had passed the site of the Plann brick and tile works and coal pit from which a branch line had connected to the Busby Branch from the south with nothing to indicate that it had ever existed.

A short distance on and a crumbling embankment could be seen crossing a nearby field on our left, leading from another closed pit and the site of the Plann miners' row, now demolished. A low ridge of hills blocked any distant views to the south and in the side of the hills were more signs of former coal pits. The bridge over the Garrier Burn, however, was still intact and to the north, beside the bridge, were the crumbling brick piers of an old viaduct. It looked as if it predated the railway and must have been part of a tramway to another long closed mine.

Ahead lay a road bridge. Beyond it the narrow track widened and was used by farmers to access their fields. Rolling pasture with cattle grazing contentedly, led to Southook Farm. A few scattered hillocks, old spoil heaps, were the only link with the past. To the north of the bridge had been miners' cottages - High Southook Row. To the south of the railway had been another miners' row. They served the Southook Fireclay Works and Colliery. Southook Potteries made glazed urinals and other bathroom fitments. The glaze was renowned for its quality. The head office, also closed, was to be found alongside the railway at the junction of the Dalry Line and the Glasgow and Kilmarnock Line in Kilmarnock. It still survives, the factory and colliery beside the Busby Branch with its distinctive tall chimney have gone - all that remains are fields. The sidings which lay to the east of the factory and also served Paddocklaw Colliery had also disappeared. The factory survived the closure of the line for a short time. The land has undoubtedly been improved by the removal of decaying industrial eyesores but the change has been very dramatic - a savage but necessary ripping away of the past.

The track headed towards Springside, a short distance ahead. A narrow metal bridge replacing the railway bridge crossed the Garrier Burn and we passed a small wood. Beyond it to the north lay the spoil heaps of the Muirside Colliery and to the south another crumbling embankment crossed fields to link up with the former railway. This spur lead to the Busbie Pits and formed an extensive network. Before Springside another route joined the branch line linking the Busby Branch to several pits - Springhill and Cauldhame. There were sidings just before Springside where these pits passed their coal onto the railway.

The Busby Branch then passed through the village of Springside, a bridge crossing the line, with the halt being located to the west of the village in a shallow cutting. The bridge has now been levelled. The Springside Leisure Trail started at this point and a tarmac path snaked away towards Dreghorn.

The first break in the route occurred as the trail reached the outskirts of Dreghorn where the trail led up to a roundabout. However, if you follow the road west for a few yards and then go left down a minor road the former railway route is picked up again at a set of steps from the minor road down to the New Town Trail. Near here the Perceton Branch, opened on 26th June 1848 and which served many local pits - Capringstone, Perceton as well as Perceton Fireclay Works, headed northwards. A small section of the Perceton Branch can still be seen on the other side of the bypass by the Annick Water.

Capringstone Bridge is then crossed. A modern metal sculpture of sun and rainbow, just beyond it, adds to the trail but of the Broomlands pit and sidings which branched at this point there was no sign.

The railway then headed towards Dreghorn Station which consisted of a single platform and a signal box. The site was beside Station Brae, which the railway crossed by a level crossing. Beyond the level crossing were sidings. Only some rotting sleepers used as a fence suggest any connection with the railway. The coal board used the sidings along this stretch to store coal wagons. Broomlands Miners' Rows were to the north-east of the station.

Dreghorn, once a mining village, is now part of the expanding Irvine New Town. In recent years new housing estates have changed the character of Dreghorn. At the top of the Station Brae there is a distinctive octagonal church. Across the road from the church is the Dunlop Memorial Hall. John Dunlop, who invented the pneumatic tyre was born in Dreghorn. At the turn of the century, Lord Eglinton led the local fox hunt along Station Brae. How times have changed.

The trail then crosses a low-lying area prone to flooding. Playing fields are passed before a rail bridge, Broomlands Bridge, over the meandering Annick Water.

Another mineral line, to the Montgomeryfield, Oldhall and Shewalton pits veered south, just beyond the bridge, roughly where a path exists today. Montgomeryfield Pit was opened in 1890. The railway then entered a long cutting. At the turn of the century this area was still open countryside with the area to the south of the track known as Greenwood, formerly Templelands, with the Templelands Woods further to the south. Miners used to race their greyhounds in this area. Templelands Woods had gone by the turn of the century and miners rows were built in this area shortly after. Now a modern secondary school, called Greenwood Academy is built on the fields of Greenwood Farm. The pupils use the steep slopes of the cutting as a quick exit from school, referring to the slopes as 'the steepies.' I wonder how many realise what conditions were like in this area in the past or even of the existence of the railway. The only memory appears to be a story about a 'ghost train', which it is claimed can still be heard late at night.

A bridge crosses the cutting at its far end and the trail continues beyond it for a short distance before it reaches a roundabout. The trail continues but not along the line of the railway. From here to its terminus at Irvine the route of the former railway is lost to new roads and housing developments. However the Bailey Bridge over the River Irvine used by the railway is still in existence now used as a road bridge. Nearer to Irvine and south of the railway were the Warrix Pits. The marshalling yards beside Irvine Station are now occupied by a retail park and the headquarters of North Ayrshire Council at Cunninghame House.

In a few miles the Busby Branch was a busy line, linking not just Irvine and Kilmarnock but many small mining communities. Most of the pits in the area had closed by the time of nationalisation in 1947 removing one major reason for the lines existence. The transformation of the land since the closure of the railway is remarkable with ugly scars and derelict buildings having been removed, but at the cost of breaking links with the past. Nowadays walkers along the route of the Busby Branch are increasingly unaware of the area's proud heritage and of the vital link the railway provided, but at least they don't have to endure the often terrible conditions suffered by generations of miners and their families.

A final thought. Little did those who built the railways in the area know that one of the residents of Dreghorn, John Dunlop, would patent an invention which ensured the success of road transport and helped to bring about the demise of the railways.

Main Features:

H1 **Crosshouse Station:** 399 397 North of Knockentiber where the road crosses over the disused track. Beware of guard dogs!

H2 **Cunninghamhead Station**: 369 414 Little remains.

H3 **Montgreenan Station:** 339 434 Private residence.

H4 **Lugton Water Viaduct:** 328 438 Biggest viaduct on the branch.

H5 **End-of-section walked:** 315 444 Turn left onto the B778 to reach Kilwinning,

H6 **Dalry Junction Station:** 297 478

H7 **Southook Pottery..** 386 399 Can you spot any remains? Located just east of road bridge.

H8 **Springside Station**: 369 391 Was located to the west of the road.

H9 **Dreghorn Station:** 351 385 To the east side of Station Brae. No remains but there are a few rotting sleepers being used as a fence where the sidings were.

5 arch Lugton Viaduct (Kilmarnock to Dalry line)

Journey I

The Parallel Line

The Lanarkshire and Ayrshire Railway

The curved platforms of Ardrossan North station

Before the opening of a suitable port to export coal near to Glasgow the port of Ardrossan in Ayrshire acted like a magnet to railway companies wanting to export coal. The G&SW had the monopoly with its Kilwinning to Ardrossan branch from the main Glasgow to Ayr line. Ayrshire mine owners used Ayr, Troon and Ardrossan to export coal. Lanarkshire mine owners mainly used the closest of these Ardrossan. The Caledonian Railway was frustrated by having to hand over coal to its rival the G&SW for the final stretch of railway to the ports. There was also local business in Ayrshire from iron furnaces and chemical works which the CR thought it could gain from its rival. The need for its own line to compete with the G&SW was therefore a priority for the CR. Hence the building of what became the Lanarkshire and Ayrshire Railway, which ran parallel to the G&SW line for much of its route.

The two rival railways had reached an agreement to jointly run the Glasgow, Barrhead and Kilmarnock line. A branch from this line to Beith passed through the village of Barrmill. From here the CR built a line for the six and a half miles to Kilwinning. Known, not surprisingly as the

Barrmill and Kilwinning Railway it was extended a further six and a quarter miles to Ardrossan on the 3rd September 1888, followed a few months later with a temporary link to Ardrossan Harbour until its own pier was opened on the 30th May 1890 at Montgomerie Pier.

With the opening to Ardrossan the company became known as the Lanarkshire and Ayrshire Railway with the Earl of Eglinton as its Chairman, pleased to promote the use of Ardrossan Harbour. The line ran to the east of the G&SW lines passing through remote countryside until it reached Kilwinning and then travelling north of the G&SW line through Stevenston, Saltcoats and Ardrossan with the siting of its stations not being so favourable as its established rival.

Further tentacles into G&SW territory followed with a branch to the steelworks at Glengarnock and Kilbirnie on the 1st November 1889 with the opening of Glengarnock High Station and south to Bank Street, Irvine on the 2nd June 1890.

Fierce competition for business benefited local traders, who welcomed the breaking of a monopoly. The downside was the lack of co-operation between the two companies which resulted in expensive duplication. Indeed such was the determination of the CR not to share revenue with the G&SW that it built another line into Glasgow from Giffen (south of Barrmill) in 1903 so that it would not have to share revenue with the G&SW on the Glasgow, Barrhead and Kilmarnock Joint Line. In Ayrshire this meant that even the Beith Branch, which the CR jointly owned anyway was partly duplicated with a track being built to the south of the Beith Branch from Lugton as far as Giffen Junction. This completed the construction of the parallel line and underlined the determination of the CR to provide its own line into Ayrshire.

The CR could now carry its own coals to Ardrossan. A further consequence was an equally intense rivalry for the limited steamer traffic to Arran, Ireland and the Isle of Man operated by another Caledonian run company, the Caledonian Steam Packet Company .

Despite the construction costs, the CR venture was well-supported and indeed encouraged by local interests and initially the L&A was a success but with the building of Rothesay Dock at Clydebank in 1907 much of the coal traffic was diverted from the L&A.

The decline was rapid and by 1932 the line had lost its local passenger services, with the closing of the stations although some excursions used the line for a few years more. (During 1930 the section between Barrmill Junction and Giffen Junction, which connected the joint line to the L&A was lifted but was relaid by the end of 1950.) Goods traffic continued but had stopped by May 1950. After the second world war, the building of a short spur between the rival lines at Ardeer allowed the continued use of Montgomerie Pier until its final closure in 1966. (Nowadays all that is left of the CR challenge is a track to the Royal Navy Armaments Depot at Giffen from Barrmill.)

There are three stretches of the L&A worth exploring. These are from Lugton to Barmill, from south of Giffen Junction to near Kilwinning and from Saltcoats to Ardrossan Pier. The stretches in between Kilwinning and Saltcoats have been largely built upon.

Lugton to Barrmill

This section is about three miles in length and was the final stretch of the L&A to be built. In Lugton the abandoned L&A line is easily found near the abutments of the rail bridge over the existing line between Kilmarnock and Glasgow. A walk south along the A735 until the first farm road on the left provides the means of reaching the line. Nearby the branch line to the RNAD leaves the existing railway line which meant that at one time there were three railway lines within a few hundred yards of each other!

By a series of embankments and cuttings the line passes under farm bridges as the track curves west towards the substantial eleven arch Lugton Water Viaduct. Closed to the public, the Lugton Water does not provide a major obstacle and the high embankment on the far side is soon reached. The L&A must have invested heavily in this the last section of the L&A to be opened.

The embankment leads to a house and lorry depot at what was the site of Gree Goods Station. Infilling of the track has removed signs of the railway but it can be seen again beyond the road bridge over the line. On the other side of the A736 there has been heavy dumping of earth where there were sidings. Skirting this area the abandoned line heads towards Barrmill along a deep cutting. The line to the RNAD can be seen to the west and beyond that whisky bonds.

A minor road is carried over the line on a three arch bridge. The line to the RNAD draws closer as Barrmlll approaches. The line for Beith left at this point. A few hundred yards along the Beith line was Barrmill Station. The station site is now a heap of rubble. Just before the L&A passed under the Barrmill road were the Giffenmill sidings in what is now used as a dump. The railway then crossed the Dusk Water by a seven arch stone viaduct known as Giffenmill Viaduct before linking up with the present line to the RNAD depot.

Given the need for two railway viaducts and several road bridges over the line, you do have to question the need for the line when there was a jointly owned line running very close to it. Half a mile to the south of where the two lines joined are the deserted platforms of Giffen Station. Heading east from near the station was a tramway to nearby lime kilns.

The L&A now headed south towards Kilwinning with the branch to Glengarnock High Station veering to the west at what was known as Kilbirnie Junction. The first part of this branch is now used by the RNAD. Beyond the extensive depot there is little trace of the branch.

Giffen to Kilwinning

This section is about four miles in length.

At a road bridge over the former L&A line, a quarter of a mile south of the RNAD we began our walk towards Kilwinning. It has to be said that we chose the wrong time of year. November rain along with herds of cattle had turned much of the route into a quagmire. Many cuttings had to be skirted keeping to the higher ground at the side where conditions were slightly better. Martin who was accompanying me was soon covered in mud. I fared little better! Another visit a few weeks later, however, made us more positive about the route and the beauty of the surrounding countryside.

The first site of interest was reached at the abutments of the missing rail bridge over the B707 near Auchenmade Farm. Beyond the road two platforms remained of the Auchenmade Station and to the east signs of sidings. Around Auchenmade Station there were various quarries and to the south beyond a road bridge was Auchenmade Brickworks. Now the brickworks are covered by woodland.

A deep cutting which was walkable for most of its half-mile length led to Lissen Sidings where a minor road had crossed over the railway. The site was a sea of mud. Power lines carrying electricity to the Roche factory at Dalry now followed the track of the disused railway. Further on at a road bridge from which the western approach had been removed along with part of the bridge we looked for signs of an old mineral railway from Lylestone Quarry about half-a-mile from the L&A line. As the mineral line approached the railway were located the Lylestone Brick and Pipe Works, now long disappeared.

Ahead lay Kilwinning with the buttressed clock tower of the abbey, clearly visible when we hit the final obstacle - a barbed wire fence with very unfriendly signs. The enjoyment of many can be spoiled if explorers of the old lines fall out with landowners. Frustrating as it was I took a detour to Kilwinning. I did spot, however, the bridge that carried the L&A over the disused Dalry to Kilmarnock line. Later I found where the railway entered Kilwinning by a seven arch viaduct over the River Garnock. Only a short stretch remains, house building having encroached on the line. We had reached the end of the second stretch of the old L&A line that still exists. The L&A station in Kilwinning was located to the east and slightly to the south of the present station and was known as Kilwinning East. No sign remains of it or its sidings which were situated at the corner of Dalry Road. The railway passed under a road bridge at Howgate and the path of the route can be seen in a park to the south of the former station site. It was here that the branch to Irvine veered away to the south east.

Saltcoats to Ardrossan

This section is about two miles in length.

The L&A headed south-west from Kilwinning crossing under the main Ayr line and under the Byrehill Junction to Dubbs Junction line which links the Ayr line to the Ardrossan Branch forming the base of a triangle with Kilwlnning Station at the northerly point. From there the line veered west. Near where the L&A crossed over the Ardrossan Branch of the G&SW line both companies' lines to Ardeer branched with the L&A branch line taking a more circuitous route. The L&A line then kept to the north of the G&SW line.

Stevenson, Saltcoats and Ardrossan on the Clyde Coast are known as 'the three towns'. Modest in size they still contained nine stations at one time. On the L&A line there were Stevenston, Saltcoats, Ardrossan Town and Montgomerie Pier. The first L&A station on this section heading east from Kilwinning was at Stevenson, later called Stevenson Moorpark in LMS days and then Saltcoats North and Ardrossan North before the pier was reached. The 'North' part being added after the creation of the LMS and to avoid confusion with the G&SW lines. The stations had gone by 1932 although some traffic continued to the pier until 1966. On the G&SW line there were also stations at Stevenson, Saltcoats and two in Ardrossan, one in the town and one at Winton Pier. With the opening of the line north to Fairlie yet another station was opened in Ardrossan called South Beach which was between Saltcoats and Ardrossan Town.

The G&SW and the CR were anxious to gain business from the Nobel Exploslves Factory at Ardeer (eventually part of ICI). Both built lines to the factory with the G&SW opening a passenger station at Ardeer which was closed In 1966. The L&A had to resolve a dispute with the Nobel which threatened harmonious relations when under their rail bridge a large puddle formed causing problems particularly in frosty weather and making it difficult for carts to use the road. The factory blamed the bridge, the L&A flooding from a local mine which had just closed.

The abandoned L&A can first be seen where it crosses over the A738 near to "Harvies", a leisure centre. The sandstone abutments are distinctive although a new bridge for pedestrians has been added. Looking back towards the sea the remains of a sandstone beam engine house can be seen beside a small loch, the engine being used to pump water out of local mines, a sign of this area's coal mining past.

It has to be said that this walk does not require walking boots and rucksack, indeed local residents might think you strange as they use the former railway line to get to shops. However when the railway was built there was far less housing and parts of the track were in open countryside. Two low road bridges cross the line and then a third higher road bridge. There are few links to the railway past.

A little further on houses have been built along the line. Near here was the site of Saltcoats North Station. The line is then lost for a short distance but can be seen again next to playing fields located between St Andrews Academy and Ardrossan Academy. To the west of Ardrossan Academy a long section of cutting still remains where there have been brave attempts by the school and local conservation groups to establish a nature trail. Along the cutting which can be quite muddy the track continues to head towards the pier. Near the end of the cutting the rail line to Fairlie and Largs crosses over. If you walk to the end, where the line is blocked then you have to retrace your steps for a short distance. Beyond this section new housing again distorts the scene and it is difficult to trace the line.

The view from the final road bridge over the L&A shows how much the scene has been transformed. Looking back there are no signs of the engine shed, the goods sidings or the signal box since new housing has covered much of the area. Looking towards the sea, the curving platforms of Ardrossan North Station are still visible but the station buildings and the oil tanks have been removed. It was a bleak end to a railway which is becoming just a fading memory.

The L&A was created out of intense rivalry and its fate was sealed when docks were opened further up the Clyde reducing demand for the Ayrshire ports. Given that the G&SW line was established earlier with more favourable locations then the L&A was always likely to be the loser. That was the way it turned out.

Main features:

I.1 **Lugton:** 410 522 Start of the first section of the walk.

1.2 **Lugton Viaduct:** 404 522 Closed to public. Gree Goods Station is next to the A736 at the end of the high embankment leading from the viaduct. This is one of three major viaducts over the Lugton Water - the others being on the joint line to Barrmill and the Kilmarnock to Dalry Line. There was also a railway bridge over the Lugton Water on the Doura Branch (see Journey I)

1.3 **Giffenmill Viaduct:** 368 512 Beyond the viaduct was the junction of the L&A line to the joint line.

1.4 **Giffen Station:** 360 505 The station can be viewed from the nearby road bridge. There is evidence of sidings to each side of the two platforms. Take care to keep off the track as there is still the occasional train on this line.

I.5 **Road bridge** over minor road from Barrmill to Kilwinning: 355 498 Start of second section of walk

I.6 **Auchenmade Station**: 342 484 Platforms remain along with evidence of sidings.

1.7 **Lissens Sidings**: 327 470 Only for the enthusiastic - very muddy!

I.8 **River Garnock Viaduct:** 303 443 Accessed from the aptly named Viaduct Circle. The viaduct is now part of a long distance cycle route which connects to a minor road to the north. The Garnock Valley Walkway also cuts across the south end of the viaduct.

I.9 **Kilwinning East Station:** 299 434 Demolished but with a building known as Caley House constructed on the site. The design of the new building has won several awards and was planned as self-catering flats for young people.

I.10 **Bridge over A738 at Saltcoats:** 254 414 Start of the third section.

I.11 **Ardrossan North Station:** 231 426 The site with its curving platforms remaining can be viewed from nearby road bridge.

Journey J

More Lost Branches and Forgotten Stations

In planning this book I quickly realised how extensive the rail network in Ayrshire once was. In this section I have tried to give some information on the history of lines and stations which I have not included in the other journeys. Some are well worth exploring.

The town of **Ayr** joined the railway age on the 5th August 1839 when the Glasgow, Paisley, Kilmarnock and Ayr Railway opened from Ayr to Irvine. The original station in Ayr, Ayr North Side Station, was just north of the river where the MFI car park is today and just to the harbour side of the former Darlington Church now the base for Borderline Theatre. Eventually the railway was extended across the River Ayr from this point in 1899 to form a harbour branch on the south side and the piers of the bridge can still be seen today. There was also a branch along the north side of the harbour to join up with the many sidings at the North Pier. From the 1st July 1857, Ayr North Side was only used for goods.

With the opening of the iron works at Dunaskin, the High Street was getting clogged up with carts carrying iron ore and lime in the morning to the ironworks and bringing pig iron back in the evening. A more suitable site for a station was required even if it wasn't so close to the harbour. On the 7th August 1856 a temporary passenger station was opened, known as Ayr Townhead (or South Side) and from 1st July the following year the station was made permanent and became known simply as Ayr Station. Opening this section from Falkland Junction to the new station involved the building of Tam's Brig where Prestwick Road crosses the railway. Ayr Townhead, however, opened onto Kyle Street which was also found not to be too suitable and it closed to be replaced by the present station on the 12th January 1886 and the Station Hotel on the 1st June 1886. The two stations were separated by only a few yards.

Newton-on-Ayr Station remains in use, albeit boarded up and was opened on the 1st November 1886. There had been another station in Ayr called Newtonhead Station which was opened on the 1st October 1864 and shut less than four years later on the 1st April 1868. I was unable to locate it on any map, but it could have been on the same site as Newton-on-Ayr Station. There was also a wooden platform called Belmont Halt, situated at the level crossing at Belmont. It was probably used on race days for VIPs attending the horse racing, when the race track was situated south of the river beside what is now Old Racecourse Road. It closed around the turn of the century. There were sidings on the west side to supply local coal merchants. There was also a signal box at Belmont but it has been removed in recent years.

The Monkton and Annbank Branch was opened on the 3rd March 1892 and linked the Glasgow to Ayr line to the Ayr and Mauchline Branch near to Mossblown Farm. It was used for goods and minerals and never had a passenger service. Situated along its three mile length were several mines. To the north of the line was mainly open country when the line was built, but is now occupied by Prestwick International Airport.

The Monkton and Annbank Branch left the main Glasgow to Ayr line just south of where the recently opened Prestwick International Airport Station has been built. Development of a car parking area for the airport has removed most of the remains of the branch line where it joined the main line although a small stretch can be seen to the seaward side of the Shawfarm Roundabout.

New flats have been built along the disused line in Prestwick, and with the building of the Shawfarm Industrial Estate few signs remain of the branch in Prestwick. The Glenburn Pit (officially known as Auchencruive Pits 4 and 5) was located where Shawfarm Industrial Estate is today next to the airport. The Glenburn Pits extended out under the sea. Expansion of the airport runways had cut across the branch line beyond the site of the Glenburn Pits.

An observant traveller along the bypass can spot a short stretch of the line to the west of the A77 near Clune farm, where there were sidings next to what had once been a bridge over the road. Building of the bypass has removed any signs of the abutments. On the east side the line can be seen crossing a field heading on an embankment towards what was once a coal bing. Memories of the smell it produced as you travelled along the road remain an unpleasant memory for one prone to car sickness. Nowadays the hill is landscaped and the smell has gone along with any trace of the mine responsible for the bing, the Auchencruive Pits number 1,2 and 3 near Mossblown which lay to the north side of the bing. The branch passed between the bing and the colliery before entering a deep cutting from which it emerged to link up with the Ayr to Mauchline line near a farm bridge over the line.

There were no stations on the branch. Monkton Station was situated on the main line north of the Prestwick Airport Station, where a road bridge crosses the line. No sign of the station remains and the site is occupied now by a siding to the BP Aviation Fuel Depot. Monkton village lies about half-a-mile to the east of the station .

The route of the present railway line in **Troon** was once known as the Troon Loop Line. A more direct line, which was latterly known as the Troon avoiding line passed through Troon, running from north of the Barassie Carriage and Wagon Works passed a goods station next to Marr College and ran across the site of the Municipal Golf Courses in Troon joining with the loop line at Lochgreen Junction south of a road bridge over the line. The route remains a pleasant short walk and is easily traced. The first station in Troon was near Dundonald Road, next to Marr College, and was opened in 1840 it eventually became a goods station. It was replaced by the present station, more centrally sited on the 2nd May 1892. On approaching Troon Station from Ayr an embankment veered to the left, just before the station, leading to Troon harbour. The harbour branch was also connected to the railway further north at Barrasie. Today nothing remains of the Troon Harbour Branch.

The Duke of Portland's **Kilmarnock and Troon Line** from Troon to Kilmarnock is of considerable historical interest. Although a tramway using horse drawn wagons the line was Scotland's first public railway and contains probably the world's oldest surviving railway viaduct at Laigh Milton across the River Irvine.

Recently restored, you can walk across the four-arched viaduct which can be accessed from the nearby Laigh Milton Mill. On the west side of the viaduct was the Fairlie Coal Pit, long closed with any trace removed, although the soil seems very black. From here the old tramway can be followed as far as the present railway. Upstream between Laigh Milton Viaduct and the present five arch railway viaduct stood a timber built viaduct. A small section of the embankment leading to it remains on the Kilmarnock side.

The route taken by the Duke's railway is followed by the present railway apart from Milton Viaduct where the tramway looped north crossing the River Irvine half-a-mile downstream and in Kilmarnock where the tramway diverged from the present railway near to St Marnock's Depot close to Rugby Park the home of Kilmarnock Football Club. The training pitch beside the stadium was where the sidings were once situated.

On the Troon to Kilmarnock line were two stations and both have been closed. Drybridge Station at the east end of a long straight stretch of railway track over Shewalton Moss, was so called because the road bridge crossed over the 'dry' railway as opposed to a 'wet' river. Gatehead Station to the east of the level crossing in this small village has also been closed.

Between Gatehead and Kilmarnock a mile east of Gatehead, the **Fairlie Branch** left the line crossing the River Irvine and serving coal mines in the area south of the river. It opened on 26th February 1849. Little exists north of the river but from the site of the bridge across the river the line can be traced crossing a minor road and heading south. In good condition the Fairlie Branch veered east in a wood about a half-a-mile south of the bridge over the road. A network of lines served many coal pits in the area. One of the most interesting diverges from the Fairlie Branch in the woods to the site of a bridge over the road near Templeton Farm where it abruptly stops. Surprisingly there is no sign of it continuing beyond this point even in maps dating from the turn of the century.

The **Gatehead and Hurlford Line** left the Troon to Kilmarnock Line near Gatehead. There was one station on the line called Riccarton and Craigie Station with sidings to the gas and electricity depots. Nothing remains of the station today which never had a regular passenger service. The line continued eastward to Bellfield Junction where the line split with one branch linking to the Kilmarnock to Carlisle line at Kay Park Junction known as the Riccarton Loop. The other branch joined to the Darvel line at Mayfield Junction near Hurlford and is described in Journey G.

Today little exists of the line from Gatehead because of the A71 Kilmarnock to Irvine bypass. The railway still extends, however, from Kay Park Junction to the site of Bellfield Junction at Riccarton where Scottish Oils have a depot.

Kilmarnock retains its station, opened in 1843, which is now a listed building and to the east of the station there is a fine 23 arch viaduct.

The Caledonian Railway were responsible for extending their line from Kilwinning to a station at Bank Street, **Irvine** which opened on the 2nd June 1890. There was an intermediate station built at Bogside. Despite encouragement and even plans to open a station next to Ayr High Street the CR never extended the line to Ayr. The Irvine Branch was single track. Bank Street Station was closed to passenger traffic on July 28th 1930 and to freight on December 30th 1939. Latterly the train from Kilwinning East to Bank Street consisted of the engine and a single carriage and was known as the 'Riviera Express'. It was never busy.

The Doura Branch was originally a waggonway used to carry coal from the Eglinton coal fields to Ardrossan on horse drawn carriages, which eventually became a mineral line and was incorporated as a statutory railway, joining the Glasgow to Ayr line at Dubbs Junction south of Kilwinning. Passengers were also carried on this line from Dirrans, which is to the east of the River Garnock, to Ardrossan and this service can lay claim to be the first 'train service' to link with boats in Scotland.

Between Dubbs Junction and Dirrans was the site of the Eglinton

Ironworks which lay between the Ayr to Glasgow main line and the River Garnock. Beginning production in 1846 the furnaces dominated the surrounding countryside for eighty years, overshadowing the nearby Eglinton Castle. This may have upset the Earl of Eglinton but he needed the money produced by the coal mines and ironworks to pay off family debts, some of which were caused by the famous Eglinton Tournament in 1839, an attempt at recreating medieval jousting between knights which attracted record crowds but which was marred by poor weather.

By 1840 the Doura branch had been linked to the Ayr line and with the need for coal the Doura Branch was extended east with branches to North and South Fergushill Farms with many coal pits feeding coal to it. Eventually it connected to the Perceton Branch. It ran close to the nearby Kilmarnock to Dalry Branch for much of its length and helped to keep freight traffic off it.

Today the site of the iron works is an industrial estate. The route can be traced from the pedestrian footbridge over the River Garnock which originally was the railway bridge. The line followed the path now taken by the New Town Trail to the nearby A737 passing through the Dirrans and can be picked up on the far side where it enters Eglinton Country Park running parallel to Bannoch Road. At Corsehillhead Farm the line crossed the road and passed through woods. From here the line is lost as it crosses a field passing close to the old coal bing of Moncur Pits 4 and 5 near to Eglinton Kennels. There are views towards the solitary remaining tower of Eglinton Castle and in the background the peaks of Arran. To the north of the road bridge over the Lugton Water an older bridge can be seen which may originate from the time when the route was a waggonway. It is possible to follow the route that the line took although much of it has disappeared. An overgrown railway cutting cuts across the Millburn Drive entrance to the country park. A short distance further on there is a stretch of embankment and an old rail bridge over a stream near Auchenwinsey Farm. A further stretch of the route is found in nearby woods and the remains of Sourlie Depot are located. On the south side of the roundabout the route then becomes part of the New Town Trail as it heads towards Girdle Toll. Incidentally the standing stones on a nearby hill are not ancient they have only been placed there recently and are from an old quarry nearby.

On the lines that remain a number of stations have closed. Many of these have already been covered. On the Ayr to Glasgow line the halts at Gailes and Bogside have gone. To begin with Bogside Halt was used only on race days but from the 1st June 1894 it was opened for continuous service. There was also a Bogside Station on the nearby L&A branch from

Kilwinning to Irvine which opened four years earlier.

North of Ardrossan the G&SW extended the track in stages to West Kilbride, Fairlie Pier and then by a half a mile tunnel to Largs by 1885. Fairlie Pier and its station have been demolished. Fairlie Station has a special siding for the loading and unloading of nuclear waste. Largs almost became a "lost station" when a train crash in 1995 reduced most of the station to rubble. It is now being rebuilt.

South of Ayr, Maybole Junction Station situated at what is now known as Dalrymple Junction, was closed in 1859 at the time when the junction was renamed. Dalrymple Station, Cassillis Station between Ayr and Maybole, Kilkerran Station, Dailly Station and Killochan Station have all closed on the line to Girvan. There was also briefly a station serving Crosshill which closed in 1862. Many of these stations served the small coal field in the Girvan valley stretching from near Kilkerran to Killochan.

The Ayr to Mauchline Branch has seen the closure of Auchencruive Station, Annbank Station, Tarbolton Station which was situated a good distance from the village and Mauchline Station.

A branch to **Beith** left the Glasgow to Kilmarnock line at Lugton and was a joint line run by the G&SW and the CR. The line still runs as far as the former Barrmill Junction to the east of Barrmill. At the junction the present line continues towards the RNAD at Giffen. However the line between Barrmill Junction and Beith Town Station closed on 5th October 1964. The station site is to the east of a road bridge over the former line in Barrmill. The station building with its single platform has been removed. Near to Barrmill there was a tramway to the north which went to Dochra Quarry. The rest of the line is easily traced towards Beith as it runs close to the B706. The site of Beith Town Station, however, has been redeveloped.

Between Dalry and Johnstone was the Dalry and **North Johnstone Line** which branched form the Ayr to Glasgow line, north of Dalry at Brownhill Junction and headed to the west of Kilbirnie Loch and Castle Semple Loch. It is now closed and some of it is used for a long distance cycle route, an encouraging development. Most of the route lies in Renfrewshire and I have therefore not included it.

Every part of Ayrshire has connections with the railways and while some of the memories are fading as branches and stations have been closed, there remains much to remind people of the past. I hope that the journeys described in this book will encourage you to explore Ayrshire and to bring to life those fading dotted lines on the Ordnance Survey maps marked "dismantled railways".

Main features:

J 1 **Ayr North Side Station**: 337 223 The trains appeared to pass through the station buildings to reach the bridge across the river. A line ran along the north side to connect up with the Harbour Branch.

J 2 **Belmont Halt:** 343 199 This area is now very built up.

J 3 **Monkton Station :** 349 277

J 4 **Troon Station** (original stations): 332 312 The buildings remain.

J 5 **Laigh Milton Viaduct:** 383 369 A casting of part of the original plateway is displayed on the bridge.

J 6 **Drybridge Station:** 359 364

J 7 **Gatehead Station:** 391 364

J 8 **Fairlie Branch** - site of viaduct over River Irvine: 399 365

J 9 **Riccarton and Craigie Station:** 426 365

J 10 **Eglinton Iron Works:** 302 424

J 11 **Gailes Halt:** 323 356 Near the golf club

J 12 **Bogside Halt:** 309 403 Glasgow to Ayr Line

J 13 **Dalrymple Station:** 348 156

J 14 **Cassillis Station:** 328 131

J 15 **Kilkerran Station:** 297 044

J 16 **Dailly Station:** 261 022

J 17 **Killochan Station:** 221 006

J 18 **Auchencruive Station:** 373 241 There are still sidings near the station site for use by the MOD.

J 19 **Tarbolton Station:** 440 250

J 20 **Mauchline Station:** 497 265

Abutments of viaduct over the River Irvine (Fairlie Branch)

Bibliography

The books that I found most useful were:

Discovering Ayrshire, John Strawhorn and Ken Andrew, John Donald Publishers Limited, Edinburgh

Ayrshire The Story of a County, John Strawhorn, Ayrshire Archaeological and Natural History Society, 1975

Scottish Railway Walks, M H Ellison, Cicerone Press

The Romance of Scotland's Railways, David St John Thomas and David Whitehouse, David St John Thomas Publisher

The Glasgow and South-Western Railway, 1850-1923 The Stephenson Locomotive Society, 1950

A Regional History of the Railways of Great Britain, Volume 6, Scotland The Lowlands and the Borders, John Thomas, David and Charles

Forgotten Railways - Scotland, John Thomas, David and Charles

British Railways - Past and Present No19 South West Scotland, Keith Sanders and Douglas Hodgins, Past and Present Publishing Ltd.

LMS Engine Sheds Volume 7 The Glasgow and South Western Railway, Hawkins, Reeve and Stevenson, Irwell Press

Mining - Ayrshire's Lost Industry, Guthrie Hutton, Richard Stenlake Publishing

The New History of Cumnock, John Strawhorn, Published on behalf of the Town Council of Cumnock, 1966

Pictorial History of Cumnock, compiled by Dane Love, Alloway Publishing

Pictorial History of Darvel, compiled by James Mair, Alloway Publishing

Pictorial History of Newmilns, compiled by James Mair, Alloway Publishing

Pictorial History of Galston, compiled by James Mair, Alloway Publishing

Among Thy Green Braes- A Guide to Cumnock and Doon Valley District, edited by John Moore

Drongan, The Story of a Village - published by Cumnock and Doon Valley District Council

Garan 1631 to Muirkirk 1950, Thomas Findlay, 1980

Gently Flows the Doon, edited by John Moore, 1972

The Dalmellington Iron Company, David L Smith, David and Charles: Newton Abbot

The Story of Ayr by John Strawhorn, John Donald Publishers

Auchenleck by Dane Love, Carn Publishers

The Lost Railway Lines of Galloway, Alasdair Wham, GC Books, Wigtown

Other sources of information were: Eglinton Country Park, Dunaskin Heritage Centre, Carnegie Library, Ayrshire Archaeological and Natural History Society Collections, Volume 7 and *The Duke* the magazine of the Ayrshire Railway Preservation Society.

Tunnel under Auld Alloway Kirk

Acknowledments

My thanks to Martin for his companionship on the walks and for his enthusiasm; to Sheena Andrew whose encouragment and interest in the project I greatly valued; to Kay Stevenson for illustrating the text and preparing the maps; to my wife Christine for her help in checking the text; to Richard Scott, one of the last railwaymen to work the Golfer's Line; to Cameron Sharp, Ranger at Eglington Country Park; Jane Simpson and those who helped at Dunaskin Heritage Centre; to Margaret Beattie, Frank Beattie, Fergus Gibson, John Geals and Anne Teaz for their help. Finally thanks to Scott and Graeme.

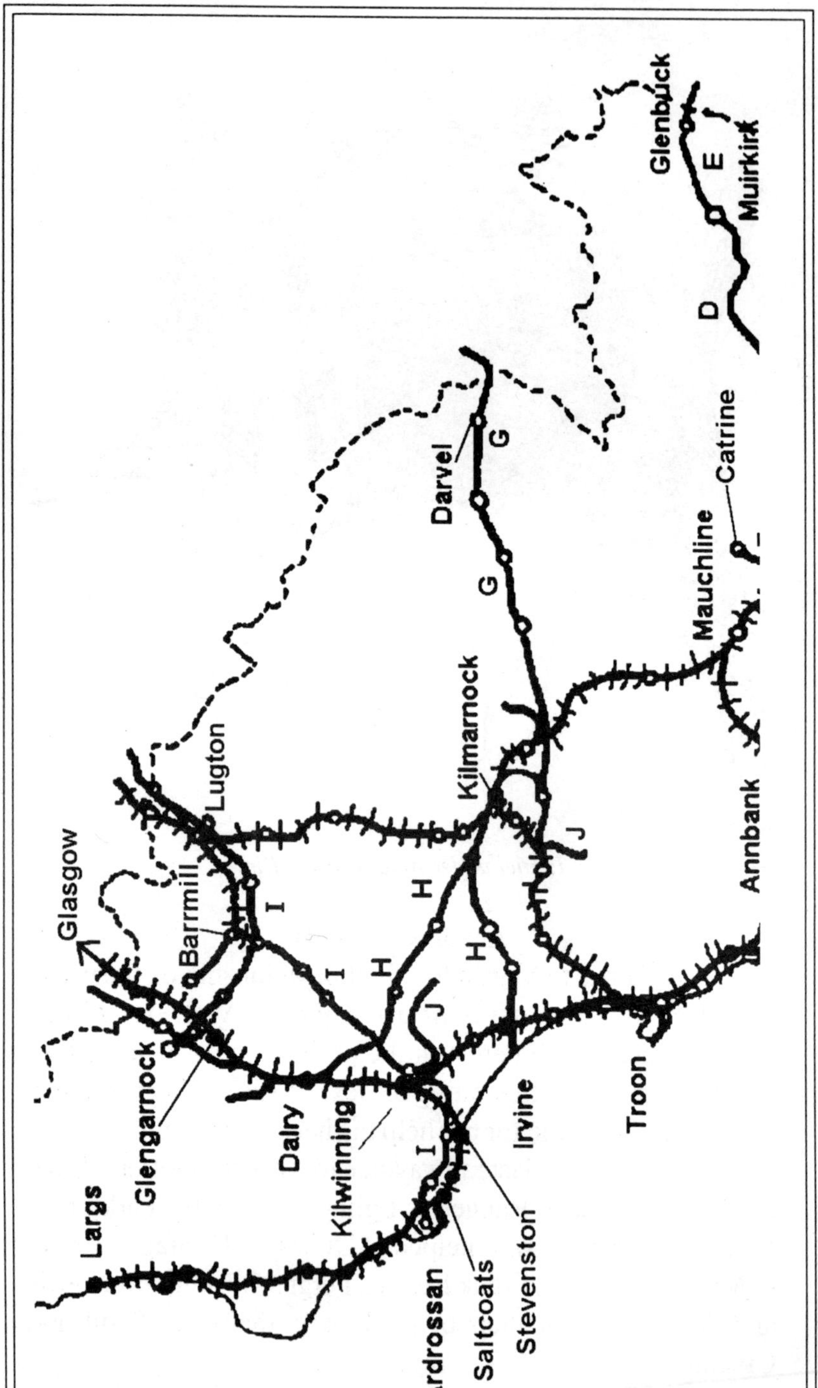

Glasgow
Largs
Glengarnock
Barrmill
Lugton
Dalry
Kilwinning
Ardrossan
Saltcoats
Stevenston
Irvine
Troon
Kilmarnock
Darvel
Mauchline
Catrine
Annbank
Glenbuck
Muirkirk
D
E
G
G
H
H
H
I
I
I
J
J

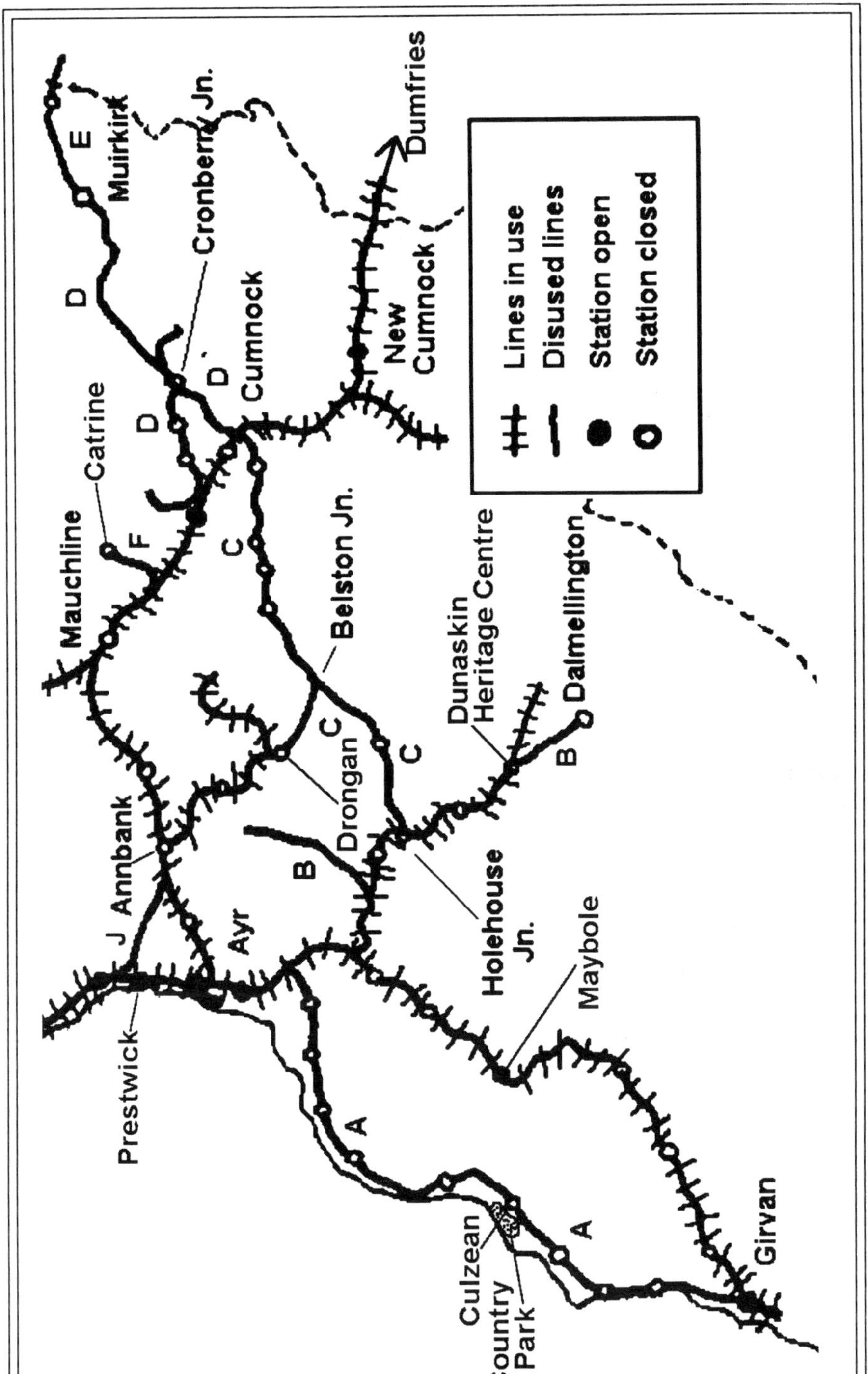
Prestwick
J
Annbank
Ayr
Mauchline
Catrine
F
D
Cronberry Jn.
Muirkirk
E
Dumfries
Cumnock
New Cumnock
Belston Jn.
Drongan
C
B
Holehouse Jn.
Dunaskin Heritage Centre
Dalmellington
Maybole
Culzean Country Park
A
Girvan
Lines in use
Disused lines
Station open
Station closed

Published by

G.C. Book Publishers Ltd.,

17 North Main Street,
Wigtown. Scotland. DG8 9HL
Tel/fax 01988 402499

email: sales@gcbooks.demon.co.uk
website: http://www.gcbooks.demon.co.uk

1997